Reactions³

Ne

THIS EXCITING ANTHOLOGY OF THE UK'S BEST NEW POETS ACTS as a listening post for anyone interested in contemporary poetry. *Reactions* showcases work by up-and-coming talent; those who are at first collection stage or moving towards it. It is published by Pen&inc, a new press based in the School of English and American Studies at the University of East Anglia. *Reactions* draws on talent from UEA and the rich writing community of Norwich and the region, but not exclusively: its open submissions policy has attracted writers from around the country and further afield.

Reactions is edited by Esther Morgan, a freelance writer and teacher. Her first poetry collection, *Beyond Calling Distance*, is published by Bloodaxe (2001).

'Contemporary poetry has been called a business, even an industry. Really it's none of those. Neither is poetry "a scene" in which careers can be advanced and the personality of a poet discussed in the Sunday reviews while poetry itself isn't adequately printed or reviewed. Poetry is a calling, a difficult and thorny path. It's the trial, failure, and re-trial of the senses and the imagination, a place where it's hard to get something even half-right, and where there are only the rewards of making. I think *Reactions³* signals a turning point: in the imaginative verve and hard-won rigour of the work; in the informed and informing discrimination of what's chosen; and in the passion behind the project: the need to release to new readers fully-realised poems that are not only enjoyable, but mysterious and intelligent. Maybe *Reactions* shows poetry stepping forwards from the media's hubristic shade and returning to its senses and, better still, to its readers.'

– DAVID MORLEY

'In the words of one of its poets, *Reactions³* "stirs the inside out of life." This vital new collection of work insightfully demonstrates poetry's power to stir everyday life into something altogether "other" through the imaginative impulse. Abundant in humour, travel, dresses, lists, Tupperware and urban plain talking, this collection deals with the contemporary lyric and the urban utterance; with issues of identity and memory, exemplifying another of its poet's notions that "Belonging is complex."'

– ANDY BROWN

Reactions³ New Poetry, edited by Esther Morgan
Contributing editors: Andy Brown, Vicki Feaver, Alison Fell,
Michael Mackmin, David Morley, George Szirtes.

Published 2002, by Pen&inc, at the University of East Anglia,
Norwich, NR4 7TJ

A CIP record for this book is available from the British Library
ISBN: 1-902913-16-7

Managing Editor: Katri Skala
Design/Typesetting/Copy-editing: Julian p Jackson
Cover Image: Will Pearson <will@digitaldreamworld.co.uk>
Press, Publicity & Events: Sara Wingate Gray

Distributed by Central Books, 99 Wallace Rd, London, E9 5LN

Reactions³ is typeset in Hoefler Text

Printed by Biddles Ltd, Kings Lynn and Guildford

Reactions[3]

New Poetry

Edited by Esther Morgan

At the University of East Anglia

Acknowledgements

MANY THANKS TO THE CONTRIBUTING EDITORS WHOSE EXPERTISE and advice are much appreciated: Andy Brown, Vicki Feaver, Alison Fell, Michael Mackmin, David Morley, George Szirtes. Thank you to Lawrence Bradby for his editorial assistance.

Thanks to the staff of English and American studies for their enthusiasm and practical support, in particular Sally Bailey, Julia Bell, Jon Cook and Val Striker.

Thanks to the Pen&inc team: Emily Knee for her invaluable administrative assistance; Julian p Jackson for his meticulous design, copy reading and type-setting skills; Katri Skala for managing the project so effectively; Sara Wingate Gray for her energetic and creative approach to marketing.

We gratefully acknowledge the generous financial support of East England Arts and the School of English and American Studies at UEA. Thanks also to our supporters for the 'Train of Thought' project: Peter Bolton at the Norfolk and Norwich Festival and Jonathan Denby at Anglia Railways.

Finally I'd like to thank all the contributors for the pleasure their work has given me and the readers of this anthology.

Contents

Contents

Contents

Contents

Introduction

'We come away with our lives ...'
– 'A Retreat', Peter Carpenter

I'VE ALWAYS BELIEVED IN POETRY AS AN ACT OF RETRIEVAL, as a way of recording moments and thoughts that are important to us and would otherwise be lost. Seamus Heaney has talked about his own poetic process as a 'dig for finds', an unearthing of buried remains. Reading a poem can be like turning up a piece of china when you're digging in the garden, trying to guess the object it came from – a cup, a vase, a tile? Poems as fragments engage our imagination as we try to make sense of them. This is the feeling I get from reading many of the poems in this anthology – a vivid piece of life is presented, intriguing and resonant because it suggests the whole. The reader is made to turn the poem over in their mind like looking at a shard of willow pattern, trying to visualize what might be on the other side of the little blue bridge ... Take, for instance, Liz Almond's poems which open this anthology and which give us intense glimpses into the lives of characters beneath their 'sun-burnt skin'. Or the elderly narrator of Margaret Easton's 'Sheltered' who senses her own memory fragmenting. Or the haunting poems of George Messo which capture those tiny moments of decision that can effect a relationship or even the course of a life: '. . . far from now we'll understand/ who sent us here, and why, and what it meant to stay.'

The image of the fragment is also evocative because it suggests something broken; it speaks of the fragility of the world. The title quote is from a poem narrated by a soldier engaged in a messy retreat – 'We come away with our lives' and, it is implied, with not much else. Some of the poets here draw on classical civilization and myth to express this impending sense of decline and fall: Anna Woodford sees a modern-day relevance in the Coliseum's history of cruelty, describing it as 'the bottom falling daily out the world', whilst in Jo Ezekiel's poem 'The Mermaids of Atlantis Speak', the reluctant agents of the city's destruction lament its fate amongst 'the scattered bones and tumbled cooking pots'. As Julian Stannard puts it in his poem 'Peace', this is the 'Narrative of rubble'. In the light, or rather darkness, of the last twelve months, it's not surprising that no one is sure of the ground beneath their feet.

*Reactions*³ is also full of questions about the problems of identity and community which seem particularly relevant in a world where the political elite are ever more concerned with enforcing unity. After a summer of flags zig-zagging across the High Streets of the land, it is useful to be reminded in Joel Lane's poem 'The Local Truth' that 'Belonging is complex.' Joel's territory is Birmingham which he explores with a subtle sense of that city's different communities, sounding a wise note of caution against over-simplification. Matt Nunn echoes the diversity of the same city and, by extension, the country, through his risky amalgamation of different registers and tones: as he warns us in 'Shipping Forecast', 'Don't touch the Bay of Biscay with a barge pole/as it is chocka with a gospel choir imploding with a cover of/ "Nice one Cyrille."' These poets know that language as much as land is a matter of belonging, or more often, division. Lawrence Bradby makes this clear in his satirical poem 'And Now an Address from the Speech Protection League (Norfolk)': 'Dialects cause cunfooshun: thass nuffun noo;/why can't the furriners talk like we do?' Many of the narrators and characters in *Reactions*³ are outsiders like 'The Trampy Men' of Brian Johnstone's disturbing poem. They ask, along with the speaker of Adrian Slatcher's 'My Alien Problem', 'Is it that I am so strange?'

There are also many poems here which look at the problems of belonging within the context of family – I loved Ross Sutherland's energetic repudiation of familial constraints in 'Dear

Grandma and Granddad' and the charged sense of estrangement captured in Roy Blackman's description of a family photograph in which the elaborate positioning of the subjects' bodies suggests the deeper emotional ties and tensions between them. The complexity of shared blood and history, of our contradictory desire to both belong and be free is beautifully expressed in Paul Batchelor's 'The Tale of the Davy Lamp'; the father in the poem belongs to a vanished mining tradition, his former life as invisible as the bulldozed and landscaped slag heaps. The uncertainties of the future and the secrets of the past come together in the poem's final image: 'The slippers I place before him make/the dot at the bottom of a question mark.'

This poem is preceded by a quote from William McIlvanney which ends: 'And the best you could do was survive.' This is a quality which the strongest poems have; they may be fragments, but they endure, stubborn as the ancient worked flints that are ploughed up like bones in the fields I can see from my window. I've chosen the poems in *Reactions³* because they seem to me to retrieve language and experience from their daily corruption in the media and the mouths of politicians, to be the true evidence of the moment.

Esther Morgan
Oxfordshire, 2002

Liz Almond

The Salmon-coloured Dress

She can't remember why
the salmon-coloured dress
belongs to her or she to it;
she thinks it might be Celestina's,
the one she gives to mothers
when they need to dress as daughters
growing out of all their clothes,
shedding them like lobsters
at the bottom of the sea –
there'll always be a tender phase
while the new shell hardens.

The salmon-coloured dress wears her,
wears her out with its ruched neck
and gathered skirt
that invoke her little self,
the one she had before
she built her body up,
acquired some muscle tone.
She muscles her way upstream to spawn.
No salt, although it's seasoned her,
can give her zest –
old woman, young girl's dress.

Darjeeling

I arrive on stilts
and pick my way
through green walnuts
that litter the path to her door,
my gateway to the East
next door, where words
like *dhobi-wallah*, *ayah*,
are household names.

There is Zena's gift of tea
in a miniature chest
you could mistake
for a Chinese firework
with its smell of gunpowder
and smoke.

From a Dansette
in the dining room
Howard Keel booms out
Bless Your Beautiful Hide
Hide? Like the trunk
of the elephant-god
they have a painting of in the hall;
he sticks his pot belly out
red as the Raj,
red as chilli pepper,
red as my sunburnt skin.

Game

She descends a ladder
from her treehouse
in the Blenheim Orange apple tree
whose pulley winched up tea,
sandwiches, fairy cakes and pop.
It fizzes on her tongue.
She daydreams flying to Darjeeling
where her sister's mountain hideaway
is far from the reaches
of the pet wild boar
who tramples on her pillowcase,
leaves his bristles
on the bathroom floor
and drops his piles of dung
like giant puffballs
on her daddy's lawn.

Others convert
the boar to pigskin bags
for toiletries and espadrilles;
but she can only hear his trotters
clacking up the stairs
to her bedroom with its straw
and truffles swelling
in between the joists,
a world of roots
that strangle
and fill her mouth with soil.
She butchers him.
Spit-roasts him whole.
Serves him gagged:
an apple firmly wedged between his teeth.

The Fishing Hut

He can say things
at the river he can't
say anywhere else;
pressure rises on his barometer
and what he wants to integrate
are continents apart
each body bound
by its own affinities.

She looks for new vocabularies –
of Blue-winged Olive,
tippet, stream-thermometer,
art of hand-tied flies,
science of metabolic rate
at the bottom of winter rivers.
The ball of mistletoe in its alder
speaks also of winter
though its berries are still summer green,
leaves the colour of river water,
thick, yellow, opaque.

She trespasses the verandah
of someone's fishing hut,
forces its shutters
to disclose keep-nets and lures.
She summons him up –
cutthroat trout on the rise.

Steve Barker

Shaman

I rise in trance:
a dream conjured
by pipe-smoke

and incense,
drumbeat and totem.
Tribe and temple, far below.

Bless me, Itzamna.
Five days I have feasted
only on air.

I come resplendent,
shod with hot coals,
robed in fire,

carrying a tribute of hearts.
Omens are propitious.
The forest flashes

jade and jaguar.
A bird flares on a branch
for one bright moment.

The moon's scythe
is poised to reap
an infinite crop of stars.

Elements marry in me.
A drowning stone
bequeaths its ripples

to the water.
The wind promotes
an ember to a flame.

Blood blossoms on tree bark.
I see the deer returning
to our spears,

the sky and earth
darkening, tattooed
with needle points of rain.

In Barbara Hepworth's Garden

On the beach, all the cobbles and the rocks –
chiselled by the wind, carved out by the sea –
were just preparing us for this: great blocks
of bronze and marble set out under trees.

Here sculptures grow with plants. We wander round
and feel each solid weight enter our gut,
the polished contours sweeping through the mind.
Standing before a piece that's glazed with light

we sense again the mystery of shapes.
Thoughts as deep and dark as Sibelius
drag us down now – past gods and men and apes –
to that old primal world where words failed us.

Curriculum Vitae

I have been a chronicler of the wind,
made manifest as banshee, balm or blade.

An expert on shadows and their shyness:
the way they hide from light behind the trees.

A finder of faces in the fire,
in clouds and curtains and old wallpaper.

A listener in the desert late at night
to silence at its most articulate.

A mourner for everything left unsaid
to all the planted and the scattered dead.

Alex Barr

Hilary Hahn at the Proms

I never let the violin out of sight,
she says in the TV interview,
It's like having a kid.

How tender she is, how very
fierce as she feeds it notes
like an eagle tearing prey,

hair flaring back as if in wind.
The bow bobs and thrusts
at the demanding strings.

Now we cut to a flock
of greying first violins
whose gaunt faces mask

what? Sympathetic joy?
Rapture? Envy?
(Her youth! Her altitude!)

Or the emptiness of ageing?
Close-up: Hilary's highlit fiddle.
How sleekly *it* has aged.

And the players who passed it on?
There – just out of shot.
A long phantom line

reaching back to the maker
weighing up the wood
of maple, Swiss pine, willow

andante in a forest
into whose canopy
a mating warbler is weaving music.

Night on Ithaca

The name SORRENTO (Sirentium in antiquity, Surriento in dialect)
derives from Homer's tale of the bewitching sirens.
                              – Tourist leaflet

He writhes in the warm dark
in tight winds of sheet
shakes my bed
a ripe chrysalis
aching to burst.

I free him. His wrists
are ridged and welted.
You have explained
your other wounds
not these.

He moves to the window.
Parched hands on shutters.
We beat along the cliffs
and then – Sirentium!
I start to understand.

That sapphire sea
fiery with flecks of light
lurching through arches of tufa –
His grey eyes
are old with water.

Ropes hugged my wrists.
The mast smooth to my skin
warm to my arching back
flag high at its truck
jerking and jerking

sky streaming cirrus
and song –
He turns to the night sky
the dark roads of the sea.
I stand behind him.

Look at me. Tall. Warm.
Hair loose, loose –

Go. Torn' a Surriento.

Ready for the Harvest

Needing bigger plots for more
vines, cabbage, corn, aubergine,
on the sides of plummeting ravines,
Madeiran families raise dizzy
walls of tufaceous boulders
on rock shelves to hold the earth.
They dig, plant and kneel to hook out weeds
with a thousand feet inches away.

Imagine. You could not let
your attention stray from your
children. On that rich volcanic soil
you would stare down into emptiness
appalled by the absence of
anything to cling to, facing with
each last sweep of the *foice*
the quick weeding out of tomorrow.

Paul Batchelor

The Bridesmaid

sits naked by the window, last light of a summer evening,
pinning and tacking, turning the fabric,
tailor-tacks guiding the darts into place.

Clipping the curves of the hips to ensure
the seam hangs true by the hidden cog-teeth. Cutting.
Dragging out a false stitch, turning the fabric.

The whispers: *Why such a hasty wedding?*
No doubt she wants to keep an eye on him!
The lining sliding inside-out, held flush

against the waxed silk, warm as flesh.
The looks exchanged when she walked by.
The quick precision of each scissor-snip.

Close by, a yellow candle in a jar
and a heart-shaped box of shuttles & pins.
She pauses. Lights the candle. Her reply:

It's no concern of yours. A give-away.
The flame sobs & steadies, her back bunches,
and her fingers work with spider-efficiency

over the delicate circuitry of the dress.

Nymphaeum
After Rilke

following the same
       channel for six-
teen centuries, since Romans

       worshipped the goddess
       & built a water
       shrine, the spring

          never dries
but quietly insistent
continues its debate:

       the slate lip juts
       from its beard of moss,
barters its handful of notes

       & sets echoes
stotting off the stone . . .
       to cup your hands

          & drink
feels like an interruption

Dmitri's Photographs

That's me in my uniform, my colours, my high style.
My brother there, laughing. Always laughing at something.
Here is my mother, after the war.

Here is the dancer I told you about:
beautiful, beautiful. But she was bruised,
her legs, under the fishnets: little burns, little scars.

And the others, other pictures, if I can find them,
if I can find them. The dance, the parade,
& this one: me somewhere, home from the war.

The Tale of the Davy lamp

*'They were all trapped. All they could do was wait, while the
government invented the weather, visited crises on them like
hurricanes, out of nowhere, never to be understood, and
somebody's son took ill and another took to the drink and one
husband was carried home from the pits and another took up with
a fancy woman. And the best you could do was survive.'*
Docherty
– William McIlvanney

From the dresser he takes the Davy lamp down,
& finding the brass is tarnished brown,
shines it, staring out over the dene

to where the remains of the mining site
where he worked off the endless sentence of his life
have been landscaped: he sees fields of wheat

where slag-heaps once stood (banks of coal dust
where kids would play: if you broke the baked crust
you'd sink in the quagmire up to your waist

& suffer a burn: a bone-deep blue stain).
He warned his sons: *It's not safe for bairns.*
He once saw them, in a tin bath, bobsleighing down.

He spits in the fire & sips his malt.
The slippers I place before him make
the dot at the bottom of a question-mark.

Anne Berkeley

Black Dog

The light is on over the sink.
Belleek on the dresser and jars
of dried beans and spices hint
versions of whitewash and shadows.
On the stove, a grumbling kettle.
A dog barks at the farm on the hill.

Brian's hunched over the bowl,
doing the potatoes he dug this autumn.
Windings flip from his lancashire peeler,
slither into the dark water.
He effaces blemishes, swivels out eyes,
dipping his work again and again with an ease

that gleams on his knuckles.
The dirt of the garden is scored
into his fingers. Stiffened by cycles
of lifting and planting, his shoulders jut forward
over the scalps – as if he is
shielding himself from the darkness.

Mother is calling now. The dog
has woken her. In a moment,
he will set the pan on the hob,
dry his hands and the instrument,
before going to her, where she is waiting
for help to fasten her things, *these bloody things*.

The Son

He'd always wanted to be a railwayman.
From his haunt at the bottom of the orchard,
from the first hiss or ringing – depending on weather –
to the last taste of smut as it cleared
the tunnel, he'd wanted to sport the peaked cap,
whistle up tanks to trunk water from the tower
then shudder free so pistons and pressure
played to the distance till only silence remained.

Later, he found a woman like his mother,
flashed his first-class travel pass at the gate,
swung their matching luggage up onto the rack,
and watched the landscape unravel into the dream
of his peaked cap, opening the door marked PRIVATE
onto tracks of violence and steam.

Requisitioned

In the war, they say, the Yanks hacked arms off statues,
gummed up fountains, burned rosewood in the grates
and rollerskated in the ballroom, under chandeliers.
And they were Allies. Our quarter's No. 9, with the balcony.

The ballroom's locked and shuttered. No one has the key.
Roll-eyed carvings guard the stairs – what's the password? –
mirrors echo in the hall, mahogany and vast.
No ballgames on the parterre. I told on them, so I'm a spy.

Stone ladies in the garden bare their breasts and bottoms
through the bones of a pergola like a broken tomb.
They gesture hooks from elbows, orange scabs.
I need a cap-gun, I said, *to defend myself.*

A box-hedge makes my den, refuses
to lie low, flat and square like its name.
The knot-garden's tangled, a cat's cradle gone wrong.
You must learn to make new friends.

Once, I hid inside an empty fountain,
staring at the green thing in the middle and willing it to gush.
Dried moss scratched my arms. A Vulcan screamed, so low
it made the twisted chimneys faint. I could have touched it.

No, I never hear *The Blue Danube,* the carriages at dawn.
There's no such thing as ghosts. The others will be waiting
on the backstairs with their skipping-ropes and helmets
to escort me to the basement, where the rats run free.

Old Bags

Hooded and belted
blue-coated Magdalens
weep over the rapefield

head in a bag, neck
let slack. Arms
pinned wide, they cannot
resist the wind:

it plucks a hem, fumbles
a button, a tear, tugs
at coat shreds
tatter, tatter.

Help me, says one,
help me

in someone's old uniform
out in the rain
fading into summer
lost in the tall yellow flowers.

Sad old bags
hang their veiled
faces in shame
unable to raise
one finger
at the sauntering rooks.

Roy Blackman

Study Tour

At Cumae, they grow beans in the amphitheatre;
at Paestum, wild black irises adorn the Temple of Hera,
asphodels and fumitory spread along its Sacred Way;
Cistus, Genista and Artemisia flourish
on the walls of the Imperial Apartments, Villa Iovis.

Here, at Herculaneum, streets with pierced kerbs
for the tethering of mules lead us to the College
of the Augustales. 'Thanks to Lucius,
Proculus and Julianus for the slap-up supper.'
The mud has moved the upper walls and pillars
inward. Charred beams, roof-tiles, slabs
of painted plaster, swept along. A plaster
mother tries to protect her plaster child,
their feet contorted in the heat like ballet-dancers.

Outside, we reach for the blue Italian sky,
the flowers growing forty feet above us.

Slide

His son's right hand
holds the fingers
of his Mum's right hand
tightly, while his left
pushes away
his father's right knee.

His wife's left hand
holds her husband's right knee firmly,
drawing it towards her.

With both his arms around her
holding her tightly to him,
his daughter sits
on his left knee. Both
his hands hold both her hands.

Her right hand holds the fingers
of his right hand tightly, but
her left hand holds her own right thumb.

His daughter's head
presses firmly to his.
His wife's is turned away from him.
His son's is held away from hers.

Wife, son and daughter
look at the camera.
He looks down at the ground
beyond his right knee.

All are smiling.

Lawrence Bradby

Rock

These are real stories. That's why
the evening paper plays for laughs,
to raise a smile, to draw its teeth.

A man goes to the shops, returns;
his kids are feeding toys one by one
into a hole in the garden.

The patio is going too,
each tipping slab dealt slippily
like aces from a pack.

Despite the headline yell to come tomorrow
there's no sound of impact;
no one says a word

till the kids rouse out the neighbours,
play footie on their solid lawn.
That's where the paper lets it drop –

the man holding his mobile,
eyeing the hole –
before the comedy deflates.

So we don't hear him scrabble deeper
down a contact list, each agency he phones
unprepared to foot the bill

for such an act of God
a freak of nature;
we don't hear the question

that stumbles as insistent as a toddler
round the hole's perimeter:
can you survive without some solid base?;

we don't hear the years of living delicately,
alert for sagging carpets,
jammed doors, little signs.

These Weaver's Hands

For you I gather in rush-hour's frayed sounds
hackling, combing the runs, trills and ornaments,
carding and ordering taut noise and slack
believe me

my shuttle tugs switchback yells of sirens
rejoicing in chase, leads their looped threads
between weft and warp that part
one moment

to knot down, to fasten these strings of nonsong
running their rough cords down alleys, through windows
                                        propped open
steel shutters, starling song wheezes
believe me

my cloths are an offering
stiffened and dressed with the hustle of HGV engines
of traffic-clogged one-ways, bass cones, vibrations
gathering, ordering

fabric shot through with swifts' shrieking,
the wide border, a jet plane tunnelling
out of the slow afternoon when I'll fold it
completed
for you.

And Now, an Address from the Speech Protection League (Norfolk)

Do I have to spell it out?
The whole time this mike has stood cormorant-stiff,
we haven't slipped one Norfolk word down its throat.
While you chew on that, check out these maps:
Roman army roads thrust north, to grab our Titchwells;
New Age whiners blotch our Suffolk border
claiming asylum from Babylon-on-Thames;
axe-happy Saxons yodel from the woods
chopping out new farmsteads wherever they please;
and in the background, the scuffle and grunt
of Mesolithic hunters scratching their pubic lice
and scattering flint chips willy-nilly.

Dialects cause cunfooshun: thass nuffun noo;
why can't the furriners talk like we do?

We're not demanding purity
just bare survival, our fragile dialect
a poddywriggler in the swim of language;
because there's always more who want to set up shop,
sit down and start their chatter: Beaker people, proto-Celts,
Vikings playing air-guitar, thuggish Norman overlords,
Walloons with secret ways of weaving, five foot
                                      ex-Chelsea strikers,
retired policemen, all knocking on our door
while outside Thetford the A11 waits and revs,
duelling to bring its dirty murmur
clean across the Brecks and into Norwich.

Dialects cause cunfooshun: thass quoit clair;
why can't they speak like us when they come hair?

And not just them, there's local folk, some here tonight,
who've stripped the mardle from their speech.
Even my own accent is erratic, I admit;
my years in Kent have marked me out for shame.

But dialects can save us, thass quoit clair.
We all should spend some time in prayer,

that our speech will stay on the narrow path.
Or maybe we should eat good Norfolk mud,
cram handfuls in right now, then stand
while round us the air is ripped
by London vowel sounds glittering like CDs,
and the mud leaks from our lips.

Peter Carpenter

A Retreat

Orderly? – Christ, no. Charred leaves ring
shell-holes in the woods. Children
prised from their warm pits just
howl and howl. Receding, over
there, what was ours. Family cars
gleam in the drives of two-storey,
red-tiled houses. Fruit trees blossom
in empty fields. We come away with our lives.

Hang on though, there's a kind of cheer,
a ripple of cat-calling applause from
the back of the column. Look. There
they are. Way below us, easy meat,
within range of the foremost enemy snipers
down in the land we held, seemingly
oblivious, a couple hanging on to each
other for dear life, necking like crazy, almost
motionless. They're already becoming

a dot, a myth, a joke. We listen out
for firing. Laugh them off. The idiots
who hugged themselves to death . . .
No, nothing. Come on. They're lost to us.

Little Girl Lost

A nationwide search for the little girl lost.
Do you know this face? Can you picture
the bathtime routine? Please come forward.
Call this number in the incident room.
Cast your mind back. We have her toys displayed.
Eliminate these people in the reconstruction.

Answer me, answer me. Are you an echo?

Through a mist forming around dawn in the valley,
thanks to you out there, she's been found.
You heard her calling, climbed the rough line
of stone steps to the locked pavilion, saw her
huddled shape, rang this number. Dawn, alone,
out walking your labrador. Please come forward.

Answer me. Are you an echo? Are you an echo?

A nationwide search. The incident room.
She's been found. Thanks to you out there.
You climbed the steps, looked in at her shape.
You might be a hero, claim your reward.
You pictured the routine, knew the face.
Eliminate all the others from our enquiries.

Are you an echo? Are you an echo? Answer me.

Emily Dening

Masochists

He'd tell her, nuzzling her ear,
how his heart would sink each
time he got the call, usually Friday, three a.m.,
how they'd loom under the brutal glare of A&E.
While he tongued his way down,
she'd imagine the once-neat, beaded lines
across arms, or torso, or legs
spurting, scarlet with air,
soaking his white coat, again
and again.

Reprieve

She has no need
to charm the bouncers.

All night she threads
between the press of

dragons, snakes,
a snarling panther,

the thrust of studs
from noses, tongues.

She's light as lipstick
clear as vodka

hula-hooping smoke rings
juggling pocketfuls of pills.

A wave of sound ripples
her to the starlit roof.

The chalk moon throbs.
She reaches up

easing it, like a tired
child into her lap.

Soon she will slip back
inside her supine husk

and the moon will bare
its daylight mask.

Procrastination

Today is the day for not
stopping the dripping tap
which started when you
did the washing up,
fingers white,
tightening
round the head.

Today is the day for not
putting the handle back
on the bedroom door
which flew off each
time you did,
hurtling
down the stairs.

Tonight is the night for not
altering the stereo clock
which has winked for weeks
since the power cut,
three zeros
soothing
through the small hours.

Josephine Dickinson

Your Way

I

How long does it take to reach the end of the lane,
almost stationary, frozen? You tell me 'Go
ahead and feed the ewes.' I get my jar and catch
you up, take longer than I thought. But you are there
still, moving barely perceptibly, just slightly
swaying side to side. By the time you reach the shed
the sheep are fed. You had said 'Walk on. I shall be
very slow. I shall take a long time.' As distant
galaxies cross our horizon their image will
be frozen. And when you tell me to 'bugger off,
go do the job,' under your rough gob is concern.
You often say 'Go on' but often I say 'No.'
For I like to walk with you, your way, more slowly
than the elephant, as a galaxy at the
end of time, faster than the speed of light, so you
are swinging out of ken faster than glances can
any more pass between, faster than I can see
any longer, than I can ever catch you up.

2

How long does it take to reach the end of the lane?
You are near the end as we watch the galaxies
fade, their appearance frozen in time. I tell you
'Go ahead, I'll see that the fire's OK,' as they
recede from us. But you are there still, are frozen,
moving barely perceptibly under the trees,
your dark form gathered in the shade. As we watch the
galaxies fade, just slightly swaying side to side,
by the time you reach the shed the sheep are fed, their
appearance frozen in time. If I can ever
catch you up to taste your lips, put my arms round you,
distant galaxies will then be moving too fast.
You say 'Go on' as distant galaxies
cross our horizon. Will I ever catch up with
you? The end of the universe, frozen in time
as we watch, will never be able to reach us.

3

You tell me 'Go ahead, for they will never grow
older or change. They will only grow dimmer as
they recede from us.' Then when I come up to the
lane I expect to find it bare, but you are there,
your dark form gathered, too fast for me to see. As
distant galaxies cross our horizon, the light
they emit after the moment of horizon
crossing will never be able to reach us. As
we watch the galaxies fade, which you so often
forget, you say 'Walk on. I shall be very slow.
I shall take a long time.' You often say 'You go
on,' but often I say 'No.' For I like to walk
slowly, your way, this majestic way you exist
and travel through this space on the lane by the trees.

4

How long does it take to reach the end of the lane?
As we watch the galaxies on the way back the
gob of blood glistens on the tarmac where you coughed
and although animals later lick up the blood
the dark patch stays next morning when the tarmac is
frozen. And when you tell me to 'bugger off, go
do the job,' under your rough gob is concern. I
love the way you move so slowly that your mind sees
things differently. You often say 'You go on,'
but often I say 'No.' I like to walk slowly
with you, your way, more slowly than the elephant,
as a galaxy at the frozen end of time.

Frank Dullaghan

Weathering

We've re-pegged the sky to give more headroom.
Now the storm's gone that brought it flapping down
we can breathe more widely for a while,
as if there are no edges to the air.

We watch the day light to his careless smile,
want to believe he never was away,
getting lost in the dark howl of his head.
The doctor said he'd make it. But we watched

him break asunder and the sky rip loose.
We have no notion how we put it back
when it seemed its weathered weight would tip all
of us beyond the world we'd married.

But we seemed to find a way by accident
or fear. Now he moves about with that same odd grace
that my sister's three-legged cat wore,
dipping its shoulder as if bowing at her door.

By the Hawthorn Hedge

That morning when I came down to the door flung back
and the wind lifting the sleeves of my coat, hung in the hall,

a chill entered me. And though I piled on the turf
till my shins burned, it would not go.

I watched then, as my wife eased herself through the house,
her hair, red as my own, tumbling when she stooped

to lift the baby to suckle at her breast. It would not take much.
The shock of its black hair silken beneath her fingers.

Back in the cot I'd made out of wood, carved with a knife,
it would stare cold into my eyes.

It turned old in a matter of weeks. I would not pick it up.

We buried it by the hawthorn hedge. *Let its own come*,
I said, *and take it back*, remembering the dried sticks

of its legs, the body pale as the sheet on which it lay
and my wife, open mouthed, hammering her fists against her thighs.

Margaret Easton

Sheltered

I miss climbing stairs, coal, lilac by the ditch.
I save pills in eggcups, my name is down on lists
for lunch, for baths, for an outing to the receding beach.

I get up, it's dull waiting, I wish He'd carry me off.
Again and again I disappear, I'm found
at the difficult junction opposite the post office

where I am on a list. I'm after the lilac I tell them
think of wood-pigeons building in the stand of pine,
banisters, I want to lay the fire. Irretrievable beach

banked up by bulldozers, poor nervy sandpipers
without enough shingle, ugly broken cliff
fenced off, poking with gorse root, ends of piping.

There are plenty of us, not free to disappear,
sat high in the minibus, each with a light raincoat,
all set. Trying to forget a ditch of lilac.

43 **Station Road**

Shops come in parades, men singly in the alley
no, to boiled sweets, then run.
Double-decker's Midland Red
I must not spit.

Watch the kerb, our turning's blind
shut the gate.
Across that's Mrs Walters on her sticks
I must not stare.

The house is brick, the twist is smoke
the garage has one bubbly diamond eye
the green front door a sunset in the glass
laburnum seed can kill.

Victor the Italian's on our bench
he doesn't have a house, he stays
he has to ask for words, he gives me stamps
I tell him how it's *pardon* sometimes, sometimes *what?*

Grandma's got a nest-egg grandpa made
in nuts and bolts, her stove's got iron legs
her evening purse a spangly catch, her promise is
all this will come to me one day.

Napkin ring initials roll, elbows off, I wait to start
won't interrupt, mouth full tongue-tied
no leftovers, finished up
manners give away, like blood.

Jo Ezekiel

Leaving the Basement

The grandfather clock with its dead pendulum,
woodworm twisting in the tables and chairs,

under a constant prickle of hessian;
secrets stowed in its folds, like larvae.

You force your way up a spiral of steps
ghosted with the sun's pale questions,

hoping you've strewn enough dust
to leave a room of sediment,

and all because your bruised ears
heard the canary's final chime.

The Mermaids of Atlantis Speak

Our father Neptune banged his stave three times:
the notes our throats made, long as ropes,
pulled the city under – if we'd refused,
we'd have been sent to try our luck on land.

By day, we squirm our emerald tails past
scattered bones and tumbled cooking pots.
The eyes of skulls are plankton caves.
With every hour, the pillars weep more dust.

We won't stay here by night. We know of sharks
that trail a stench we're scared to name.
The city swarms with echoes. Far beyond,
neon jellyfish pulse upward, searching.

Stuart Flynn

Temples

We could not send them away entirely,
the gods, so we did the next best thing,
and lured them into objects
that we created. They seem to obey us,
judging by their silence,
but we have no way of knowing.

Perhaps one day, someone or something
will drive them out before their time,
and even make them speak.
Then their former temples will be empty,
home only to owls and other night-birds,
but we cannot send them away, the gods.

Think Carefully Before You Answer

Is there someone you would rather be?
Now, before you get all excited
and shout a thousand different names,
read carefully the instructions
set out below. Having made your choice,

you must actually become that person
in every way. Think what that might mean;
you might love to have someone's money
but not want to be ninety-five years old
and married to a young gold-digger

you never see. Someone else's beauty
perhaps hides an empty skull, and fame
might be bought at who-knows-what cost;
I am sure you get the idea.
If you thought of someone with wisdom,

virtue or supreme genius,
they might also have their faults,
but then you wouldn't be playing this game.
The rules should all be clear now, so:
is there someone you would rather be?

Your Time Starts Now

Why do bad people have good fortune
while good people often suffer?
Is it because:
     a) the universe makes no sense;
     b) in this way, those things often valued
    are shown as in fact worthless,
    when given to the least deserving;
     c) this problem has never been answered
    completely satisfactorily
    and one lifetime is far too short to try; or
     d) all of the above.
Make your choice and then stop work, please;
what you don't know now you never will.
You there, yes you – stop work, I said.

T. K. Fountain

Anatolia

Hills of brown earth, seeming   so like sand feels,

with feet sliding down the climb up,   the soon-gone tracks

we only imagined leaving.

And from this dry, grassless earth, little more
                    than a stick, barren of leaves:

less gold-green than   simply yellow. We spoke of this

nearly to the point of arguing, save   that it was too incidental,

at late day in this place.   This tree more waiting for life

than alive itself, which was   my point –

the one you   outright dismissed.

The sun setting, blocking our way   with light, we waited

in the frame of what   would have been an apartment, now left

for the plains.   Beneath the cool stacks of cement,

we searched the corners   for clues of those before who
                                                            waited on evening.

In our ear, the click/scrap/click of our shoes
                                                            and the wind whipping

through block-shaped holes   waiting still to be windows.

Origin of Memory

For as long as we need them, they are ours:
those eight days on the south coast – as much ours as anything.

Sun: Tight heat on our skin, its weight was with us
              even in darkness, our careful movements
              not to irritate stinging flesh or mar the sheets
                              – intention in lieu of passion –
              and the shower at cold trickle,
              just enough to wash you off me.

Water: The rocks from which I edged myself to sea
                              – graceless, slippery , sliding –
              you jumped, plunged, proud of what I could not do,
              with the Mediterranean slapping up sea around us
              and the depths I feared too much to swim for long.

Time: Each other's constant presence: by day we shared
              the space of ten feet, by night, less, when not relaxing
              in books or my evenings at dusk through old Datça,
                                                    roaming
              streets of stone too narrow for the car you insisted
                                              on driving.
              Near dark, wandering, in search of something
                                          beyond me, others
              who must have been here before us.
                                    I was too full of myself
              (and you perhaps) to notice anything but expectation.

No revelation — just more of the same.
The same longing from those days
(as from you)
for the unreasonable.

And I pictured you reading near a window to catch sight
of my returning exactly as I had left. Everything
comes back, rushing, to this idea

       – this remembrance –

of what was once real, irrevocably
lost if existing at all.

Still, in that blue room, by that square open to night
sky, with warm air slapping at curtains, and
the buzz of insects hiding in grasses – as if calling

       This is it   *not yet*
       This is it   *not yet –*

there you will be as long as I need you.

Ivy Garlitz

Big Brother

It would be heaven,
like being reborn,
big in the frame, knowing
it's natural for people to point cameras at me,
and be riveted by my every change.

I'd be admired for outlining my stardom
as a model and personality.
And everyone could see it,
they could virtually taste it.
They'll watch me as I sleep.

When my friends go
I'll be certain I'm more loved.
I can't lose:
no matter when I get the call to leave,
my family will be lined up to hug me,

I'll have spotlights
and the cheering I always knew was there
though I couldn't hear it,
a wired new best mate slipping her arm in mine,
guiding me to room-sized archives of my finest moments

and views of the world aching from my absence.

Lies
After Chris Ware

You'll meet the person who you've imagined
making you perfectly happy, complete.
Your past will shut tight; your problems all binned,
your faults disappeared, the sex will be sweet.
You'll have no more need or wish to dream.
Things will get better as time hums by.
You'll never be lonely or want to scream.
You'll have the satisfaction when you die
that you'll be remembered for eternity,
given as an example to future lives
like themed nature pictures that reek of tea
and chimps clutching mugs, dressed as waking wives.

Number 1 in a series of Lies and Their Purpose.

For a collector's album send proof of purchase.

Marilyn in Korea
After an exhibit in the Smithsonian Institution

The stage of planks
is covered with wires leading to her,
to her four mikes, all poised on their stands
to catch her singing,
not the four men in red jackets and bow ties,
their hands clasped behind them, mouths open,
backing her up.
The countable rows of GIs

and the MPs watching with them
all look freshly shaved.
They hold up to her
Kodak Hawkeyes and Reflexes,
flashes with tin auras.
This portrait was taken by a medic
called by his buddies to a good view
of her black strapped dress,

the silver hoops at her ears and wrists,
the silver brooch pinned to her bust,
her open-toed pumps, bare legs.
Her hair's more unnaturally yellow
against the grey hills and overcast sky.
'After this moment,'
the curator's caption declares,
'She becomes a controlled commodity.'

My father isn't here,
not in the rows in the shot, or the band,
or in the tents, or in the hills above the stage.
He refused to see her
and missed his chance to be part of history,
a head barely cropped from the bottom,
a pair of hands at the margins,
captured pressed together.

Anna Garry

The Weight of Words

She speaks a special type of Braille
air knots, smoke strokes,
the necessity of touch.

She tells you about wallflowers,
hollyhock, instances of shade,
thrushes' eggs, a blackbird's beak,
the golden inhibited song.

Alone she'll trace pebbles, malachite,
crystal, the pleasure of hard grain,
fractures, shale, steep slopes,
the inevitable slide of scree.

Should you look into her eyes
you see she walks on eggshells,
knows the pain when sound's held back
how breath is clamped by fists,
the feel of sandpaper on skin.

She has the weight of words
cushioned in each palm.
She lets them all float free.

Harvest

She counted the stubble of straw
watched chaff rise over a field
saw insects running for their lives
and the oblivion of men pausing for milk.

She sipped the heads of sweet clover,
waited quietly for a bee to sting.
She kept frogs cool, dripping water
into their drying pools.

At dusk she chased daisies in the meadow
nose down, eyes squinted for
the last curl of pink.
She'd lie on her back staring at the sky.

She collects mushrooms at midnight
waits for a burst of fireflies
wishes for a moon on the wane.
She's alert for the flick of bats,
catches shadows in the trees.

Margaret Gillio

Waking

This is a moment
yet to happen.

It could be the moment I wake up
in our bed, hearing you
in the kitchen cooking your breakfast.
You are singing until you
sense me staring
from the doorway.

It would be a blues song.
A man singing
good-bye to his wife
and I would know this song
is for me, even though
I don't know her,
the woman
you've mistaken me for.

I've scripted this scene in many ways.
I like this one best: I'm watching you
as through a telescope
of objectivity, looking for signs
that you have left our past
to move into your own
unscarred future.
I want to carve a space
into the silence.
A room for myself
within a shared future.

This isn't memory, yet.
Anything can happen
because I only imagine
I know who you are.

I am not watching you.
I am not standing in the doorway.
I am not yet awake
because I am afraid to move.

You may break my prophecy
by walking from the kitchen
into the bedroom.
I feel you bending over me,
your weight on the mattress.
It is a moment that I want so badly
I'm certain it won't happen.
But objectivity
is closing in
as you bend over me.
You pause to listen
to my breath, like
a mother listening to a newborn
asleep in its crib.

You pause just long enough
for me to crawl back in time,
back inside that woman
you first loved.
You kiss me on the cheek
and then on both eyelids.

I only pray we know who she is,
this woman waking to you.

Ancient Chemistry

A man pleased
a woman.
The man was pleased
because it was his manliness
that pleased the woman.
The woman was pleased
because she led the man
to self-pleasure
by guiding him along
the path to her pleasure.
So they knew this:
pleasure together.
And he was none the wiser.

Chrissie Gittins

Iguana

I hadn't moved for days,
at night I simply put my feet up on the chair.
I would focus on one point in the garden –
the hole in the fence where a knot had been,
till all my muscles held a stillness born of strength.

At first my legs melded into one,
the green scales spread to yellow towards my thighs,
I rather liked the curl ending in my tail.

With feet the longest journey could begin.
I clutched the shelf-edge with my toes
and turned towards the painting on the wall.
Reflected on a mouth was *my* flabby crown,
my one black eye rested on his chin.
I ached to lick the surface of the paint,
to catch its roughness on my hoary tongue.
I envied the illusion of smoothness on his skin.

I will in time, of course, avoid the isolated tree.
Prehensile though my tail may be
I'll choose the lower branches,
I'll listen out for moths,
and faces placed on pillows
in the surge of morning light.

Instructions, L'Uliviera

There is a window in the bathroom
which will steam over when you take a shower.
Only then will you realize it has slipped in its frame
to leave a strip of clear clay hills and russet rooves.

For two days you will rue the lack of towels.
The other side of the *arte povera* wardrobe
is opened with a tiny hidden hook.
The towels lie there quietly in deep and subtle piles.

The bed will bring the comfort of sleep
and the certainty in dreams
that your friends are capable of betrayal.

On the first night you will hear Italians banging
and shouting at the door in a necessary release of resentment
after years of thoughtless tourist parking.
You will, in fact, have left plenty of space
for the man and his wife to pass.

The woodburning stove will, in time,
warm the winter from the walls.

But as the pipe runs into the bedroom
it will scorch the sheets, the duvet and the mattress
while you are having wine, olives and conversation
with the couple from Norwich next door.

On the third day there will be sunshine,
on the fifth, snow.

Elizabeth Taylor's Nose

If these photographs were a pack of cards
I'd know how to lay them side by side in families.
Is this Queen with the floral frock
the mother of this baby?
Did this Jack of Hearts with his hand on the bonnet
of a Ford Anglia marry the girl in chiffon?
Had they moved to this white house
by the time photos came out in colour?

I've never seen anyone who looks like me,
not a mother or a brother or an aunt.
When I lay in my cot the staff touched my nose.
'Like Elizabeth Taylor's,' they said.
My name from them was Liz.

Chosen by new parents, to live in a solid house
on the borders – my name from them was Laura –
I shelled peas, broke off sticks of rhubarb,
learned to love mackerel.
I changed the date at school, defined the weather,
counted the petals on countless yellow daisies.
Academic work came easy.

With one birth certificate saying born in Scotland,
a second in Arbroath, I grabbed my passport.
My aeroplane flew low on a detour
from a foreign city, and there below in miniature –
the sheep and spinneys,
the drills and trellis of my Lanark home.

When there was enough life between I went looking –
too late to show my mother my content.
I read the cause of death –
heart attack at fifty.
I had her down for teenage pregnancy,
another family,
a possible half-sister or a brother.
At least a conversation where she could tell me
if this was Uncle Ted or Auntie Flo,
if this was really *her* covered in rose petals
from head to toe.

Taking Alice to the New British Library

Alice studied in the vast domed room in Bloomsbury on Saturdays,
in time spared from schooling students for exams.
She sat once in the wrong chair,
only realizing when she started adding to someone else's notes.
No chance now of sitting in the wrong chair
as we wheel her into lifts, along ramps,
between glass caskets of manuscripts and maps.

Now we wonder at a medieval world,
cerulean sea, golden mountain ranges
bunching like caterpillars –
all parallel and crawling East.
Unnamed rivers and deltas magnified
enough to flood the land,
lakes which look like guesses,
placenames listed inside coastlines –
a tight fringe of landings.

North Africa is almost right,
Spain and France are true,
Asia melts south, indistinct,
like icing on a crystal cake.
The countries grow out of each other,
sharing frontiers, only Britain floats alone.

Alice would like a boat, but more than this a plane,
where she could sip chilled wine,
and plot hinterlands through the bleary window pane.

'N'

The first two shops had 'T's' embroidered in white
and 'M' in royal blue.
'N' took three shops to find.

An empty carousel of yellow ponies
spun through the rain.
The Sally Army played bright carols in the square.

I found your three handkerchiefs rolled in their box like bolsters,
hanging between the socks and serried ties.
They were what you'd asked for.

Will these flat stitches ensure they stay in your room?
Or will they join the chain of chattels
passing between each patient?
You have so little of your own –
a geranium,
a poster of a biplane,
a photograph of your comrades reunited on a runway.

And this card, which brings you greetings
for a birthday close to Christmas –
Boats at Royan, Samuel John Peploe.
Will you remember kicking a ball on that beach,
eating frites around a table just beyond?

Now that your skin is a shammy,
you only feel sunlight through glass.
Or see the shapes it makes on walls
as it beckons behind a bolted door.

John Hatfield

The Collared Dove

Your soft fashioned flask
of dove shape,
your serpent head and berry eye
so calmly poised on the decay
of the washhouse roof. The sky
tiled up behind you
in cold glazed blocks.

Keep still, and tell me,
slant-elegant, dusk-filtered cream –
how black is the great room
of night after you fold
head beneath wing?

The Animal on the Roof

Indigo shoulder, night-sky leaning on glass,
a woman's head silhouetted, absorbed in herself.
She is stitching, stitching,
so the cat's stealth thinks in silk
as it slinks
under her angular chair
tilted like Cassiopeia
above the frost.

Keeping Quiet in the Heart

The winds dragoon across our hiding places
hurling messages from the cloaks of invisibility
and doubling as carriers of the foist and reek of pestilence
across our crouched rooftops, where we, within,
sit as Russian dolls within ourselves and will not listen.

We need these still retreats, cannot let in
such shocks and infamies; we say
to ourselves they must all be rejected,
are no more than the bellowings and smells
of bulls, angry in rotting yellow hay –
not relevant to us, that we have no time.

To think in stilled pictures and to count at intervals
is our lot. Such gusted legends and barbarities
are to us intolerable, ripping out slate and heart
and custom without acceptable alternative.
Roaring as they do into the funnels of our own
retreats, they shake our resolution yet make us hold.

Yannick Hill

Knowbody

Her wrong mind
must stop trains
in the countryside.

Screech; then quiet.
Her agency like frost
on the dark fields.

The conductor says
it is cold outside
and there is someone

on the track. And.
My name is mentioned,
relevant as a flare.

The rescue is a dream.
She is asleep now.
She makes a good sound.

My mind must stop.
The winter trees
are just breathing.

Nature Programming

A deep-sea fish with teeth that flash so
that they warn,
and golden eyes doused in looking.

Back on the surface,
someone is trying to tame the dog
with photographs of the sea.

I imagine the golden eyes
of the deep-sea fish
on the face of the dog.

This new creature
remembers a time
before it was tamed,

when the moon shone
before the sun:
What a time for swimming!

I take the dog for a walk
and his play-biting
draws my blood sometimes.

Whoosh

I throw myself from standing;
the fall is like a trick
and it hurts;

'Pity is in the wrists,'
you say,
when it is too late.

The snow slope
is like the muscle
we use for sleep.

I slide like a note
in a pipe,
and there is no blood.

Wounds like watermarks.
I'll stay
for the ice storm.

You say, 'Get up,'
(as if I weren't listening)
'and leave the sledge where it is.'

No

On the other side
of the glass
dark happened,
answering no.

I stepped onto the lawn
as if onto my back;
my head felt like glistening
peat looks before it is burned.

With branches from my trees
I was clobbered
in the night cupboard
until I could only walk.

I remembered me to me
by knocking my head
and bleeding and walking.
The bracken divined and cracked.

Found in a bramble bush.
Hands helping and hitting.
Warm blows, as under wings,
ripped and held.

Patrick Hobbs

Homecoming

As I read your message I realize
I don't know how to come home
to you; the roads I have used before
are too safe,
I forget to see
and always meet you three doors away
from the house I know to be ours.
This route may take me longer,
and if I arrive across country,
scarred, unshaven, smiling
in a torn coat,
then understand
love is no more than a wound
from which we never recover.

Telephone Account

Nine weeks later my telephone bill
remembers our every word
and silence, a note of your code,
your number, the time, the day;
all the seconds of our conversation
measured, totalled and subtracted
from my bitten account.
The figures so sharp, specific,
three pounds and seventeen pence,
as if someone had focussed a camera
through our curtains, shot
our silhouettes in black and white;
so sharp I look again to see
if some computer has numbered
all the hairs of your head
where my fingers lost count in the dark.

Normandy

Walking Saturday night the road
from Lassy to Saint Jean le Blanc,
we pass no cars, only cattle;
a nightjar whispering like a myth
toward the black horizon trees;
the remembered dust of a soldier
shot on this lane that August
when they fought a whole day
to advance a thousand yards.
Our steps and our breathing mark the stillness
like the thin passing of birds
as I gather flowers from the fence-rows
to lay them by the shy stone
his family left here like bread.
I want to tell him that the road
to Saint Vigor is now open,
the tanks and ashen snipers now hide
in histories and tourist museums;
tell him that earlier this evening
I lost at pétanque
to a beautiful girl from Prague,
and tomorrow we will cut our names
into the sand at Arromanches;
that tonight at Lassy, in the café
we have left behind, a young man
with a blonde guitar is singing.

Andrea Holland

Mariachi

is not all je t'aime and sunshine.
　　　　The old women, always old women, refusing
　　　　black lace shawls, calling it something else.

is probably from Marriage, the French again,
　　　　another funny verb, another wedding.
　　　　There is more to Mexico than meets the eye. It

is one of your favourites. Guitars,
　　　　violins, to have, to be, je t'aime. Old women
　　　　in blue dresses, keeping time to *Je t'aime*

is on the tape stuck in the stereo
　　　　of the truck as you drive through Mexico
　　　　to somebody else's wedding. Sunshine

is burning your ears and the skin around your funny bone;
　　　　arm out the window making shadows like birds
　　　　in the desert.

is not just a street band, the sons of old women in black lace shawls
　　　　at a small country wedding in Mexico. Call it something
　　　　else, your tape melting in the sunshine, call it music, love.

The Man Who Didn't Leave

is here now, in the kitchen. He is about to
slice vegetables, to help you. He wields a steel
knife – a sharp grey eye looking this way –
as he chats about his boss, a fax, and some new girl
at work. His thumb comes close to the blade
but he's on a roll; gallantly prepping (broccoli,
pepper), waving the cleaver and laughing
while you bite your tongue. He's close to being done
and you're thinking of Shylock: the price you are about
to pay for this.

Naomi Jaffa

Jury Service

They suggested wearing
poor old George's red Fez
or a pair of white gauze fairy wings
or possibly goggles and a snorkel
(in which case she must sling a large wet fish
– preferably a halibut called Norman –
over her left shoulder).
At very least she should carry a copy
of *The Guardian* or *Telegraph*, or both,
aim to look as prejudiced as possible
or potentially schizophrenic.
She could try turning up with
Repent All Ye Sinners
on a sandwich board, a bit like
the anti-meat man on Oxford Street.
Or suffer Tourettes and say *fuck* a lot.
One thing was sure though, they said:
if she wanted to be objected to
and sent home on day one,
she needed to know
the right way to go about it.

Comeback

The show starts around 5 a.m..
Outside our house, Cilla Black
of all people tugs my sleeve,
tells me she's worried
but that I must see for myself.

He sits – or rather, reclines rakishly –
on a floating perspex chair
and recites-intones-sings
through a maze of thin
curling plastic tubes,
backed by what sounds like
a dub or Jamaican reggae beat.

It's a real departure, a whole
new image. But I worry
from the rear of packed stalls
whether they'll now find him funny
or simply ridiculous. Myself,
I just can't tell.

Head thrown back, hooked up
to this complicated breathing
apparatus, his speech pulsing
in a series of clear bright bubbles,
running fingers through unnaturally
lustrous hair in a practised
'resist me if you dare' gesture –
well, I think, at very least he's back
on stage, in person, performing live.

Lifestyle

We alarm and disable
our cars in the latest
parking bays on the bridge.

We sleep downstairs
in unexpected rooms
at unfamiliar hours.
They say it is safer.

The sky is always yellow,
humming and buzzing
like an old fridge.

We've got used to
the static in our hair,
to swallowing the taste
of a sucked bunch of keys.

Kebabing is the new sport:
there are burnings
most Saturdays.

I hear my buried voice
in snatches; haven't touched
a book since they tried
erasing living memory.

Christopher James

The Collaborators

In the end it was just the two of them,
the night they stayed up all night,
drinking pint after pint of holy water.
They sank it like Czech beer – in quantity
and at length. When they ran out,
they drank Czech beer.

They spoke only to confirm their fame,
dropping words into each other's sentences
like Russian babies into sub-zero lakes.
They exchanged the typewriter like a pistol
with a spinning barrel. Outside,
the snow fell in whispers.

They told the time by the chink of the coin
in the washing machine in the next room
and listened to *The Greatest Hits of Link Wray*.
When they grew tired, they chewed their belts
and nailed a chair to the door. At three a.m.,
they began to cut their hair.

McBaird's dark ringlets fell through his fingers
as he worked. Gurney, whose hair was fair
and short to begin with, did not take long
to reach the crumbling honeycomb of his crown.
He passed the time with his impression of a man
dismounting from a penny farthing.

At daybreak, the door splintered open and
a tall man in a beige suit said: *It is time.*
On the table was an envelope of hair,
a broken typewriter and a note which read:
*The nakedness of woman
is the work of God.*

Newfoundland

Her eyes were a wilderness
of dark fenlands
        silver plated with rain.

Her face was the shadow
of a bird on the land.

Her skin was a prairie
of white bracken and hemlock.

She wore peacock feathers
and knew what they did not.

When they arrived,
they painted their houses
        brilliant white

and built miles of gold fencing
that stretched to the sea.

She kept to herself the secrets
of the earth,

and the language of the dark
but shared with them

the light and the light,
the sorrowful light.

Brian Johnstone

After Mallory

It is not difficult for me to believe that George's
spirit was ready for another life . . .
                                                    – Ruth Mallory

They search the mountain like some hillside,
some rising ground behind their home

they seek a missing child in. Strung out
like votives on an icon, below the yellow band,

each rakes in horizontal lines. A half hour
from the highest camp, they find it,

face in prayer deep into the shale, fingers
clawing at the gravel with a vengeance

he would never have: the English corpse.
A name tag stitched on what the weather left,

the fibres winnowed from the shirtback,
proof enough. The cylinder abandoned,

found jammed beneath a rock above, just
corresponds. Like breath, the question hangs

condensing in the chill. That this cadaver,
tweed and hobnail boots, made the summit,

stood there, took the photograph? The search
picks wool from layers: cotton, flannel, silk;

frayed rope from rough abrasions on the waist;
finds goggles pocketed, suggests a late descent,

the evening shadowing the snow. It finds
no camera to make him human, bring him back.

In thin air, something close to hope evaporates.

Some tokens from the jacket's folds are what
they take, then lift a cairn of slabs to lay upon

the desiccated flesh that slid off, caught
and held here. What's left they give

the mountain with a psalm. Unproven,
this is just remains again, a bag of bones

until, ten thousand feet below, the hands
receive each object, turn it to the light:

a box of matches, faded Swans; zinc ointment
torn in half; his knife; his altimeter,

smashed and dumb. And papers, folded
in a handkerchief, their eyes connect to, read

the words he carried, absent minded, to the top:
a letter in his brother's hand; a store account

unpaid, deferred till his return. From what:
this peak they know he must have reached.

And this is when, in consequence, the breath
seeps back, the bones unite, the man

steps from the photographs, flesh whole.
From faded cuttings, dotted maps of routes,

he picks his way through rocks, crevasses,
glacial moraine, making for the tent.

Shed Blue

Based on ultramarine which was synthesized in 1828,
this blue distemper covers the walls in The Bothy at
Calke Abbey – now much faded and discoloured.
– The National Trust Garden Paint Catalogue

They conjured you from base ingredients
in time to have your photograph preserved
in black and white: not quite what you deserved

but light absorbing anyway, and since
you had to make your mark it was enough
to be felt noted, if as no more than

the back drop to a rustic scene, this ham
arrangement of the stable boy, a trough,
a wooden bucket and a brush outside

The Bothy. This is where it all became
so clear that you would never shine again
but be discovered where you first were laid

on wood, which sheds you now, a faded skin,
and measures time in flakes:
so blue, so thin.

Sentience

It is as if the thoughts you measure, try to grasp,
the words you think
you have held on to, are not there

but hover somewhere out of reach;
the way those constellations
that your eye can only focus on for seconds

vanish then,
until you catch them unawares
through sidelong glances, furtive snatches at the dark

that gives them back for moments:
as the mind does,
almost without prompting,

chancing on a place as tentative, as unknown
as the night sky that I gaze upon
proportioned by the moon.

The Trampy Men

Those trampy men, the real ones, must have gone
around that time: the year the last real tram went by

bleached white in mourning. Aged just six I watched it
from the flat, up late, toes peeking from pyjamas striped

like those I saw at seven, in the grounds of the asylum,
as their wearer, agitated, moved my way. Just loonies,

we said, tipped into the bin, tipped out again to take
the air. We'd spoken to them, laughed at gestures,

unexplained remarks we only saw as different from
the norm that made me fail to understand his wave:

the quick flick of his fingernails – my learning curve.
Broken, ragged, striping blood across my cheek, it stayed,

made these the tracks I ran on now: to turn and gawp
at wierdos, every trampy man, unshaven, frayed and off

the rails. Or daft, like this, the latest one: those tin hats
that some army surplus store had sold him for a bob,

a khaki-hued pagoda stacked upon his pate. Now safe
behind the windows of the *Consul*, I twisted in my seat

to stare, to catch the buckle of my *Start-Rites*, stripe
new ox-blood upholstery, draw out whitely oozing flesh.

Chris Kinsey

Immigrants

Mesmerized by the squish of wipers,
tyres, door suctions,
I haven't kept time.

Stratford Road is one long rule,
pet shops and post offices
mark distance.

I must be getting close.

The man beside me relaxes;
all the rivers on his coat
change course.

When the drip falls from his nose
I ask directions.

With deft handwork he cuts
major junctions out of the fug,
counts off traffic lights and bus-stops.

I'm unsure of numbers,
his English struggles with names
and landmarks I don't know.

Shrugging, he smiles
I'll show you.

Gotta bus pass see
won't cost me nothing.

He points through window mist,
Sparkhill Park, very nice.
I lose track in all the trickles.

Free day today
Free day tomorrow
he chants against the pelican
crossing's urgency.

I surprise myself
and ask what he does,
Welder, factory worker.

He turns his collar up
leans against the return stop.

Thanking him

I think about my father
standing over spark showers,
Saturdays too,

coming home deaf and ragged,
swarf in his soles
scraping like spent shrapnel.

Did you make enough welds
to fuse your *heimweh*?

And what do you hear
now that the anvils are still?

Children of Parents on Crutches

set off early,
walk fast,
tease stones and cans,

pound walls,
shoot the moon
through basketball mouths.

Children of parents on crutches
meet up late.

Don't speak about it,

but score tarmac,
skate under streetlights,
deep-breathe frost . . .

These are our charms.

Losing the Scent

Walking home under low watt cloud,
eyes tracking splashed almond petals,
berberis, with its sweet scent, mugs her.

She remembers how, last year,
it seduced two girls, left them
pollen-gilded and fluttery as moths
dipping their faces into the yellow bells.

They called and she joined
gasps and laughter until dizzy
they moved on, wary of cracks in the pavement.

Approaching the corner now,
she's watchful for ambush, finds herself
in the wrong direction for home,
wandering galaxies of white plum.

Joel Lane

The Local Truth

You should never make assumptions.
They might be the Neighbourhood Watch,
those boys in combat jackets.
Keeping an eye out for crime.

That's why they're taking photographs
of that group who look like students,
who aren't from around here.
Belonging is complex. The cadet boys

are starting to chase them. Maybe
they've stolen something. They've dropped
the leaflets they were carrying
and run into the police station

to give themselves up. Don't come here
and start making judgements.
The lads wait on the quiet street.
Things are back to normal.

Soho Hill

Under the shallow curve of the flyover,
skateboarders dodge invisible barriers
and pigeons scrape fragments of naan.
The shadow follows you to the hilltop,
then burns like oil in the silver flame
of the new Sikh temple. Stone crests
shimmer as if primed to short-circuit.

Ten years ago, these shops displayed
cheap groceries and dried-out roots;
the upper windows were boarded.
Now, the street is a living catalogue:
imported clothes and fabrics, music,
videos, books. The eyes of the economy
are dazzled by every kind of light.

Among the new facades, a few blank
shells remain, half-dressed in posters.
Teenagers drift hastily from door
to door, unwilling to be framed.
Their parents keep their eyes on the road.
They know what all this was built on,
what it has cost, what it still might.

What Happened to You?

Don't show me your objectivity
like a new pair of cufflinks.
Don't show me your new cufflinks.
Don't wave your plastic in my face
like a passport without a photo.
Don't give me that knowing look.

Tell me how you couldn't find
your way home in broad daylight.
How your fist cracked like a stone
and you saw the ocean within it.
How you were a father for a week
and a baby for a long weekend.

Or tell me about going to vote
and leaving the card unmarked.
How you watched a swastika drag
its broken legs up a wall.
How the open face of a country
closed and shrank like scar tissue.

But don't give me a balanced opinion
when the truth is off balance.
Don't answer your own questions
by flicking conjectural ash
from a cigarette you've given up.
Don't confuse reason with this.

The Prison Ship

We've seen them on the staircase
holding hands, heard the whisper
of their private conversation
echoing in the narrow corridor.

They smile whenever their paths cross.
Can't they feel the harbour's rhythm,
or does it make them think of love?
Can't they smell the decay from below?

Doesn't the salt breath of the wind
dry out their little hearts, cure them?
Don't they hear the anchor chain
groaning under its flesh of slime?

The day they leave, we'll turn back
to avoid hearing their struggle
as the black water closes over them
like a duvet, rocking them to sleep.

Brenda Lealman

Break Up

The animal in her
senses the end,
waits for the
slide apart

for sag of ice
first swing of tide,
the shift of dark
grown stiff with time,

its bend, roar,
heaping out,
all fiery currents,
mad light.

Fractures scald
to melt holes,
what was thread
fine as a fish bone

through the murk,
becomes a web of shadings,
flow-ways teeming with
backs and eyes.

Hiss of wings overhead,
a peregrine drifts,
wheels, then hack
of geese returning.

On the tundra
snow sleeks to
brown, slimey
like piles at a kill.

She listens: in the hammering
another brazen beginning
always just beginning.
The shout in her.

Shelf

Someone's up there
on a shelf of cliff
above Boggle Hole

going into earth for
two hundred million years.
She'll meet devil's toenails,

snakestones, belemnite bullets,
monkey puzzle jet, the starts,
stops, deaths that have become us.

One day, we'll lie down,
squeezed out, flattened to outline
like shells or fern fronds,

our moistness, cytoplasm, all the
loops and shootlets in us, becoming
what we do not know we bear.

Weather moves over Dogger towards
German Bight, to the dim line
where you've yet to happen.

Coming Back

One Friday afternoon at three
they creak towards the surface,
blackened headstock starts to move,
giant pulley wheels are turning.

They step out of clefts, cupboards,
those who've been in earth's insides.
They come riding in the cage,
lean out to light.

They reach for mending,
try to catch someone's eye
call from where the wash house
was: no one hears.

Up above, little tubs
on wires are busy,
empty themselves into sky,
make burial places for them.

A Tom Pudding clanks by,
carries them to the dark canal.
Earth settles, grassed over,
gas moving in forgotten workings.

But nothing's ever finished:
seepage, stirrings underground.
Old Pullen the knocker-up
will wake them again.

V.G. Lee

Johnny Big Bananas

I

1942
In town, our trees are much admired;
the tallest, left unpollarded
wave splintered fingers
at departing planes.
Like hands, he said, patting
her salmon pink silk knee.
But not like Johnny Big Bananas.
She uncrossed her legs,
silently willing his hand
to travel higher.

To the East lay Everest –
dazzled I kept on circling.
Mosquito. Mosquito Merlin –
much better – a bird.
Light, free-wheeling,
built of birch plywood,
just wood and glue –
burns as fast as a shirt and trousers,
faster than flesh –
what happens to bone?

Those first few days
after 'so-and-so' died,
she walked quickly
as if speed alone
could sort the painful matter out.
Whistled *John Brown's Body*,
in defiance of meeting with
a famished wild-eyed ghost,
scoured scraps of charred paper
for disjointed words
expecting a message from
a god she was suddenly
eager to believe in.

2

1990
At Frinton-on-Sea where
the grass is kept artificially green
it feels like rain.
Predictably an aeroplane
crawls quietly overhead, dropping
the shadow of a small grey cross
onto the crowded sea front.

Away from the fuss –
cotton dress leaf patterned,
lined tortoise neck and face
make her almost invisible
as she struggles painfully homewards.
He follows behind, hankering after
the bony abacus of her shoulders
and spine. Had he lips left to tickle
her grey curls would be tickling his lips.

In Exile – 1997

The nurse, this morning, searching for a pulse
along my thin, yellowed wrist;
apropos my inadvertent remark
concerning the changing seasons said,
You have such a charming sing-song voice,
did you ever live out East?
I snickered, *Only for a few years during the war –*
but English born and bred.
Given an open field and four strong legs
I'd have cantered away, blonde tail flicking,
instead I added, *But of course . . .*
as if . . . who would imagine?
Sufficient words to give nursey the gist
that hospitalized, elderly,
losing my marbles maybe – still,
I was nothing if not a pure-bred English lady.

Later drowsing in a chair,
(I am press-ganged from bed at eight a.m. sharp),
I trot back fifty years to September 1947.
We, my soldier husband of fourteen days
and I, stand in the brown hallway
of his mother's terraced house in Smallheath.
The air seems charged with soot,
banisters gleam like a row of ebonised bones.
My mother-in-law is saying,
Tell her not to wear that hat.
Tell her working-class women don't wear hats.
Tell her, only tarts wear hats like that.

She smelt me.
I was cumin seed and curry powder
lodging in the pinched slits of her nostrils.
I left my foreign spores in the filaments
of her moss-stitch cardigans. Out of control,
in her opinion, oiling my wanton way
over the linoleum landing, holed up for days
in our bedroom where I more than made
my presence felt between the army blanket
and darned sheets. I was a tropical forest
on the move. Plumes of hot vapour
steamed from between my legs.
To save the life of her precious son,
she couldn't have placed her hand in my armpit.

Rain falls like silver fish.
I'm topped and tailed and back in bed
ready as I'll ever be for the long night ahead.
Nurse calls it, *A time for playing up
and high jinx*, which sounds as if
it might be fun, but is only her cheerful slant
on shouting, cries and senseless laughter.
When I was a child,
rain was an endless, bamboo curtain,
steam curled hot fingers
around the foothills below my village.
The temperature truly was . . . temperate.
Sounds and smells, noises of the night –
so very different. But that remains
my business.

Christine McNeill

Waiting

Spooning the fruit
she savoured each piece
before it disappeared
into her mouth,

and when the spoon was clean
she held it like an open book
or something she had worn for years –
the reflection of her nose, her lips

abandoned and retrieved
as she turned the spoon.
Her smile was special then:
as though she'd walked for miles,

had read a dozen books;
as if each step and word
had birthed another step and word
somewhere in the room.

And when the spoon was taken
she gazed into the mirror
at an open door
and said the air tingled –

as though someone
is painting my face –
and when the door shut
her face lit up:

each step, each word
invisible, unheard,
but in her memory a birth
that never was.

While You Sleep

I ring.
You do not answer.
When too much life threatens
you take to your bed.

Words ripen in your mouth
like seeds in moist earth.
Dark sentences tap into the room –
inflections so strange

that as a child
I imagined them as angels at the window,
looking at leftovers I scraped off plates.
I knew they were hungry.

But afraid to call in,
or smear jam on the pane,
to noiselessly break it and wrap me
in their thick white wings.

Your words white as angels
or the air around the Taj Mahal,
while your voice stripped to the bone
and your hand trailed over the edge of the bed.

I want to shake the walls:
an eyelid, or a strand of hair –
a sunrise plea to break the surface –
but at your end all is silent.

On my idle PC screen two blue triangles
weave in and out. Their changing shapes
a timeless placing of loss; their soothing speed
like inner rain.

George Messo

Mothwise I

For once I know we
have to live and why.

A thought entirely you,
each day makes spaces
shaped for inner things.

Tonight, a Trabzon balcony
in spring. The sky has peeled
a segment set in time.

Mothwise II

Still it is something the storm can wake us;
chords of driven rain strike the window.

We rise and thumb around the darkness,
oblique in unlit skins, and cling to it,

what love there is, close enough
to sense how far we've moved apart.

First there is Morning

The clouds in you anoint a blue mood.
And you say you woke early with a feeling
of smallness like fear, newly made. And I
in my own cocoon woke late from desert thoughts
and sky-parades, dwarfed by expansion.

So we wake at opposite ends of ourselves
in a city which is always Ankara
and the weather born in you
rises in me like fog black from the mouth
as I go down the seven flights of stairs
through the vein of a cold December apartment.

Today is not the day to leave. By some concocted chance
in a smoke-filled tea house far from now, we'll understand
who sent us here, and why, and what it meant to stay.

Hotel Paris, Trabzon
For Mustafa Kılıç
After Apollinaire

Rumour is I'm leaving.
My room is shaped like a cage
and the sun puts a fist through the window.

But I, who only want to smoke,
know nothing, and light my cigarette.

I don't want to leave.
I want to smoke.

The Orchard at Night

The walk uphill inspired you.
– Others know the world turns slow going up –
You closed yourself off from the town,
pursued by fusts and Autumn smells.

Darkness spat figures along the path.
Men with beards and suspicions
– of what they were not yet sure.
But wait. You were just an idea
of a thing they'd truly hate, given time.

Move on. Look back. Ahead,
the sky turned red behind the trees
and the mountain sang once more of home.
Behind, a future of holes you'd return through.

A comet appeared in the sky that night.
You trembled and slept.
Why had you gone there?
Didn't I say you'd be cold?

A Trabzon Orchard

Earth smells rising up.
A week of rain unbinds
a summer mountain, cools
a sense left sleeping there.

In groves, I knew him once,
coaxing fruit or yielding grass
– some esoteric scheme
to stir the inside out of life.

A man alone is almost mythic.
The city closing in could not
subvert him. And who can touch
him now, among the hazel,

lost in leaves and God?

Jenny Morris

Child at a Festival

I ride from the gloom
on a broken-backed horse.
His ribs in my flesh,
his lungs ratchet and wheeze.

A wing of mine's lost
fallen down in the dark.
This one, like a hand
waves at every response.
I don't understand
what the question might be.
Its white feathers spike
as my fingers could do.

My hair's filled with discs
of false daisies and pins
that stick in my head.
And my fist's in my mouth
to stop all the words
that might drop in the road.

We hobble and clunk
towards people at dusk.
We're looking for light
just to show where we are
and why we are here.

Lunatic Moon

Light leaks through this wall
killing shadow dreams
where my lilac mother floats.
She knocks on my heart.
Moon dust falls on her face
spoiling her violet smile
and filmy fingers.
I must lure her back
out of the night,
my true mother who faded
into bones. Her honey hair
fell down. She called
like a raven until
her breath stopped.
And then the false mother
came with her jangles,
manic lies, closing the door
on my father's voice.
Bruised moon falls
over the edge.

Stephanie Norgate

Tupperware

That summer all the women were wild for tupperware
and held parties to sell pale plastic and opaque lids.
There were tinned salmon sandwiches and sausages on sticks
and cress the kids had grown on flannels. Permed and perfumed
they danced to James Last's *Tijuana Brass*, their eyes Latin and intense,
their homemade dresses flaring round their legs. *See it seals*, they said,
it seals, keeping everything fresh, wasting nothing. So they kept
the jugs, the bowls, the cake containers. The children, up late, laughing
through the door's crack, saw nothing of big stale larders,
brown jugs standing in bowls of water, butter melting on a cool cleft
shelf in a deep cottage wall, raw meat on a square slab of marble,
or of girls who'd been hungry and cycled everywhere,
                                        who knew how to use
each cabbage leaf, each dreg of milk or lump of dough. Later
the women would snap shut a single sausage or a spoonful of jelly
and pile the leftovers, box after box, into their singing refrigerators.

Photos of K.

and I thought how through it all
someone was growing dahlias

storing tubers in boxes all winter
cutting roots to grow rows and rows

of deep red cactus dahlias
protecting shoots from frost

and someone was growing roses
feeding them with blood and bone,

and someone was buying them
from a cold lorry packed with buds

perhaps juggernauts of flowers were crossing
Europe, their drivers chatting at service stations

their hands chilled by damp stems
bags of carnations piled high

they don't unwrap them
photos of photos pinned to wooden stakes

bags of deep red dahlias
their cellophane crackling

like the papers I rifle through
for the quiet village murders we hardly notice now

if it wasn't for you
in a helicopter with Rich beside you

his head swivelling like an eagle-owl's
I'd probably be reading about the prince's mistress

how the mind refuses to settle on bags of bodies
grown row after row *they don't unwrap them*

and follows instead the journeying friend,
the trading of flowers

Outdoor Wedding in Vermont

Waiters sauté over small fires, trick
delicacies out of the dark, balance

them among pyramids of flowers.
The groom's speech. How he loves his best man.

How the Barbie bride is homely but she'll do.
Bottled laughter. Good mannered, they leave

on the dot of midnight. Fairy-tale rules.
Later the wife will wrinkle off her gloves

while racoons come out of the woods
through the sickle leaves of sweet chestnut

stepping over spiked half-opened shells
to eat canapés in their clawed hands.

Notes for a Poem

If I want to write
   about white willowseed floating in green air,
and I really mean
   my mother in a red wheelchair, borrowed from the Red Cross,
and I really mean,
   the memory of my mother, a second-hand memory,
because they told me – I wasn't there –
   'we pushed her right up here,'
in the face of ruts, flints,
   and hardcore hidden under the mud of the bridleway
or whatever name the map gives to this track,
   and instead, I write of the laminae of green leaves,
of beech, hazel, elder, sycamore,
   and look for far-fetched words, like *green earth of Verona,*
viridescent, fern-green, viridian,
   and really mean the bottle-green
without the glaze of glass,
   and the brambles, a tangled mess from apex to ground
and back again,
   that is a wood in summer, with its green mat of sound,
its flashes and ovals
   of sun wavering through the leaves' filter,
how, then, will I be writing of my mother
   and the way we miss her,
by writing about the white willowseed,
   floating through the green air in May
two years after she was here
   jolting over the rutted mud of lime and clay
breathless among
   the photosynthesizing trees?
All my notes repeat
   repeat repeat, more or less, this:

willowseed drifting through unabsorbed green
a white speck floating in the corner of the eye
or in the corner of the mind's eye
suspended yet moving quietly
among the layers of oxygenating leaves

The Phone Tower Wood

Out from under the phone towers, on quiet hooves,
    deer munch stems of Queen of the Night
before the tall, greening buds
    can ever uncup
their veined dusty crimson light,
    their pools of blood-black bruises.

It's a strange consolation to say, over and over,
    on the phone, or in pubs to city friends,
the deer have eaten the tulips again.
    On a rare evening, I'll see all three of them
cantering over the tussocky field,
    back to the phone tower trees and their humming cover.

Matt Nunn

Shipping Forecast

Baby sleepyhead, the night is buttered up
so you may Zed off and
drift into a child's drawing of a dream.

For all you spacemen creepy-crawling across the pie crust,
England is hand-stitched
together by bruises and memories of miserable moaning,
summers spent in shorts in Morecambe Bay.

Don't touch the Bay of Biscay with a barge pole
as it is chocka with a gospel choir imploding with a cover of

'Nice one Cyrille.'

Lovely Malin Head is nuclear aglo-aglo with chips dropped
from the boxing glove mitts of dead end Johnny.

The soft soap sound of the universe is more 'aaahh!' than even you
with all the fab and God-blessed kiddies gently hymning,

'Keep right on to the end of the road.'

And the Beirut obstructing the throat of Cromarty is terrorists
of the syntax spewing their mish-mash of vowels.

As we search for shadows in the dark,
the lights of Newcastle bounce . . .
Bouncing off your shut lids, strung-out truckers
F-word speed through our slowed-down minds,
screaming with cargoes of our frightmares.

Exterminate Members of Boy Bands

Pouring down the dumb-dumb bullet sky
have-a-go mourners climb inside their
onion sunset eyes to hide from the inevitable
that a child could've told you.

Chasing the profits of prophets chic-ed in used
seventies lizard skin, is like borrowing a mute bloke's
opera voice to joyfully holler of all the art
that lies sacred on the lips of creation

which leaves us deeply in the cheddar plugged into
the cul-de-sac scrubbed clean by a PM's vote-grabbing denim,
trying to catch before they're dumbed senseless the falling swirl
of gutter angels sweetly soul singing of the shite we're in.

Manzil Rising

Epically heartbroke,

floating, alone, between strands of hoolies
shoved out to sing sad straight
from their skins,

until reaching peak of where dark blares
with light fantastic and cowboys hang,
leave their horses out to dry.

Inside
Bombay twangy spills down skeletons and shirts,
as piled high priest pops more poppadoms upon the table
than there are mouths gathered.

Skunked up to brink of amazing bellybutton wisdom

'Waiter!'

speed shovels of favourite yummy munch down to
extend fabric of my soul

'And could you dollop me more side order of self-loathing.'

What a shame bloke she chose to run a billion trillion
miles for her turned out to be such a hopeless, legless

waste of fabulous teeth.

Don't worry mate
and believe me

if there is future booked beyond impending Armageddon Madras
then I shall gladly cough in full for my emotionally vomiting bombs.

Reactions[3]

On a magic naan trip
reverberating with twisted thrill, we crawl through
dishes and dirty valleys, flaming intensely immensely.

'Waiter!

shriek me up a bodybag to taxi me back to trudgery
and post me to my mother in a doggie bag,
remains of my heavenly happiness.'

It's a long long road, there'll be curries and sorrows too.

Rennie Parker

Burrow Mump, Deadened by the Sun

Windows are open to let the badness out.
Hummocked cattle slump on the seething green.

The school bus arrives. It is packed full of chairs.
A taxi leaps over the bridge and disappears.

No no no says the butterfly's flight
Doddering over banked-up nettles.

Traffic lights scream *STOP* at the empty road.
Angles of buildings cut everyone's voices down.

Betrayal in the Formal Gardens

Look at that, you say.
Are artichokes in season? I do not know.
By the topiary hedge
We should seem okay. Their finicking heads appear.
These pleasant vistas!

The long air of the afternoon
Slides down. I would rather not
Be here than there, not here, not there;
A dissociate possibility.
Such difficulty comes from not quite caring.

Between close-set hedges
An isolate pond appears. The lily flower
Sails out from the floating raft . . .
What need of you do I have?
Are you anything there to me? Was
There something I should have done, or said?

Where five lanes meet there are seven trees
An apple, and a rosebush. Choose
Yourself some thorns.
Hear the rooks cawing home.

Belvedere Park

The children in descending order of size
Stare out across the terrace towards the sea.

The boys are dreaming of murderous deeds
As Father disappears behind *The Times*.

Soiled clouds beetle overhead.
Mother resumes her embroidery, stabbing away.

The bougainvillea blooms unnoticed.
The girls stick pins in their dolls, also unnoticed,

And Roger is lying down in a darkened room
Surrounded by medicine bottles, seven deep.

Peacocks echo on the distant lawn.
Dr Benson is due to arrive just now

Bearing his latest device in a velvet-lined box
Which proved most effective at Malvern.

Ferns drift over the brick parterre
Their somnolent mist. Close blue settles around.

There will be a storm tonight, a wrecker
To set the weathervane spinning.

Across that verdure on patent feet
It is the butler Kensington who comes.

He takes a whole age to arrive
As the blue-eyed girls remain motionless.

Dean Parkin

Smokes

She rattled in his face a matchbox
found in his school trousers. He told her
they were his teacher's, borrowed
for a Bunsen burner and took to hiding them
with the spiders dangling in the shed
or wedged under his bike seat.

She noticed she was losing cigarettes,
counted them and caught him in the kitchen,
so she made him smoke the whole packet
until he was sick and dribbled a promise
with crossed fingers, resolving to find other ways.
He could always swap his dinner pass for them.

She said she could smell it on his clothes,
so he told her how much she stinks too
and she beat him, the bruises admired by friends
as he removed his shirt before he lit up
in the safety of the trees on the common,
rib cage skintight with each inhalation.

She didn't mention it again and he guessed
at some kind of victory as he stood alone
unbuttoning his shirt by a rusting sycamore tree.
But as the milky light trickled through the leaves
and the sky dirtied, winter began to occur to him
and he shivered, coughed, blew smoke.

The Family Shopping

The girl joins Mum in the bookshop, says Dad wants her opinion
    next door; a coat he likes.
Mum says no, tell him I'm not interested, but the girl wants her to
    come because he'll only ask her
what she thinks then and how does she know? So she stays there
    pleading, go on. Mum, please go,
until he arrives himself and explains. There are two he really likes,
    one's light and the other's a stiffer leather
but she says she doesn't know why he asks her about something
    she wouldn't dream of buying herself,
how you said you were coming to buy clothes and now you won't.
    It's your decision. It's up to you.
Looking for Aromatherapy, she leaves him picking over Local History
    before he circles round and tries again.
What about the style of the jacket then, can't you at least comment
    on that? But she won't relent,
says it's like Sophie asking if she should have purple hair or blue
    and Sophie agrees, adds you're like that
when Mum asks anything. You won't help me then, he says weakly
    and repeats it, this time in despair.

From an Open Window

a man is talking to the moon.
The moon yawns
and would check its watch if it had one.
Isn't there anyone interesting
to listen to at this hour?
But the moon wears its best shiny face
as the man moves onto secrets.
He tells of lovers
reduced to the size of photographs.
He speaks of friends
who have been lost like small coins.
He wonders about plans and schemes
which weigh him down like sandbags.
The moon sighs
and drifts off behind a cloud.
It imagines being a cueball
disappearing down a black pocket.
It would like to be a pink bubble
blown by a child
and snapped back into its mouth.
It wants to be a balloon
that snags in a tree
and is burst by a curious twig.
But the moon says nothing,
which is what it thinks it looks like;
a big fat zero, while the man
continues the story of his life.

Kate Rhodes

Violin Lessons

The violin-maker troubles me with his advice.
'The wood,' he says, 'must be air-dried.
Avoid the kiln, for the sound of leaves,
wind-blown, rustling.

Today's lesson is materials.
Always sycamore never maple,
spruce for the belly – it loves to curve.
Wash each joint with hide glue and care;

remember, in a hundred years' time
there may be need of repairs.'
He's impatient with me.
I must learn to hear the wood,

understand its fibre,
bite it and listen to its taste.
In my hands I must bear the ribs, the back,
the neck, as a mother bears her child.

'Listen to me,' he says, 'there will be days
when the hollowing will whittle at your life:
the notes too are trapped,
but they do not fear the stave.'

Bluebells

Men stopped giving her flowers.
In her garden, frosted and dried
the winter plants were a lifetime's
spent bouquets.

She needed to give herself a present.
A bathroom with no mirrors,
white towels to wallow in,
a tub big enough for remembering.

She had to find the perfect blue –
not iris, not midnight;
the sky's watchfulness
two minutes before dark.

In the paint shop
the young man listened carefully –
mixed lilac, cobalt, amethyst
a practised conjuror.

They saw it spin into colour
or he did, she watched
the blackness of his hair.
No grey, he must be half her age.

His eyes when he noticed her
were a quick green sea change.
'I can tell,' he said, 'when you dream
you dream of bluebells.'

Kate Rhodes

The Doorstep

I try not to go back
but I'm driven there at night,
in the old Morris
smelling of leather and fear.

My father hides under the lime tree,
yellow handkerchief leaves
wrap him in sticky cover.
He's left me on the doorstep,

marble, grey and veined.
She paid me to wipe its dirty face.
I can see inside the lion's mouth,
its copper roar *Brasso* clean.

My father has disappeared,
the car too is dissolving.
There are no footsteps.
No one will come.

Memorial

Bumpy as a crocodile's back,
the table you made wears
Spode, Wedgwood, Poole,
lodged in its resin skin.

It's heavy with food and words today.
A resting place for drinks,
crisps, condolences,
unwanted cake.

We remember as much as we can,
scatter your name on the seedbeds
until the rain pelts us with silence.
We salvage almost everything –

the wine, the strawberries,
the photos of you.
In the porch I watch the wind
tear white petals

from the clematis,
handle them roughly,
hurl them to the wall
like plates at a Greek wedding.

Jacqui Rowe

Green Guide Blues

The *randonner* man is playing
        keepy-uppy with his head
    and person-from-Porlocking
      my right brain
          as it tries
            to write
how
  when civilization invades from the West
        Tschibo and Benetton are the advance guard
    bringing promises of
        legendary soft ice cream (two flavours).
And Pappenheim
      is not a place
          in Thuringia
             on this earth,
      in the Fat Man's gazetteer
             of signs
     playfully turned round
           to nowhere, leading always
to the same waterfall (one kilometre on foot,
        allow three quarters of an hour).
And I'm saying,
    distortion and you have a special relationship,
                Tyre Man,
      leading me two stars, what the hell,
          worth the visit anyway,

away from what I want to write
about
    cobblestones and communism
                        because Mr Pneumatic
               cannot stomach hustings when
    they obscure the
               Goslar Rathaus (three stars for
polychromatic woodwork).
And I'm saying,
           why do we keep not going to Hamelin,
                           Tread Boy?
                Instead of the one star
only interesting
oldest biggest least known soonest forgotten wooden planked
          church
          in Christendom
              and Lower Saxony
                    I want to watch
       a child
          or possibly automaton
in a boot propped up by a towel.

Rite for my Daughter

If I were a spell woman,
        my caesarian hidden
            in my scarf drawer in the garter box
              within the Harrods bag,
              I would burn a ring of purple candles
              on a Thursday evening for you,
              tie pink ribbons round the tap.
Not being,
        I text the words of power: take care and let me know.

If I were a woman of the hearth,
        my half-bent fingers shaping
            dolls and leaves for pies
              against a bosom pinafored with steam,
              I would warn about the faultlines
              on your pavements where the ladders pinch,
              calculate the values of your magpies.
Not being,
        I watch the news for signs.

If I were a henhouse woman
        my broken birch twigs riddling the woods
            put out by water, ovens, easy tricks
              of boys and candy,
              I would preserve your life within an egg, within
              a fish, within a duck, within a hare,
              within a bear, chained to a trunk beneath the sea.
Not being,
        I earn and keep you warm.

Hameln

Back from church, bellows
empty and littl'un,
Grut as was said, away.
Should taken to scripture
sooner, man said,
not stuck one home
to scoff grain and go.
But more right for such
to keep fire. Left grain anywise,
more for rest on. Then was whistle
of one knew other words of
rainbow. But were Wolli only
and head soft from having crutch,
nattered about paradise
again. Had of grain
then went for Grut. Others called
others. Landlord say man
had all, for pay for rats.
Looked for then, down walls
to river learned by rainbow man
broad and wide, before just river.
Grain lay on longer, work was more.
Shade of Armun turn up
through port in robe all dagged
dyed by sheep piss, sing
regenbogen and come with.
Mardy littl'un alive.
All beat, landlord say till sink
in broad wide river. Saw ghost drown.
Liked rats ever,
never scoff grub young uns would,
kept in cradles for being with
till littl'uns were back,
born new.

Robert Seatter

The Square of the Abandoned Clothes

Following the elephants, the festivals,
we came upon all those clothes laid on paving stones
in the middle of that vast windy square of an Indian city.

Rainbow clothes: skirts, scarves, pantaloons,
thin buttoned blouses, lonely black stockings,
saris stretched out in sheets of gold-stitched purple,
tiny slips of underwear rolled into gutters like so many leaves,
a little girl's dress – something a doll had forgotten,
a shiny pair of lime-green running shorts.

Clothes filling the square, staring flatly up at the sky.
And no one there. As if all their owners
had laid them carefully down, walked off naked
to another city, found a different way of being, new words
for drapery and buttons, new words for not needing them at all.

Or as if they had thought they might return in the night,
next week, next year, and see themselves lying there,
waiting, under the moon, and decide again
that was who they were; gather the material, strange and warm,
up in their arms, smell the bodies that once were inside,
and breathe new life into them.

Runner

In memoriam JS

Maths was torture to you, round the class reading
of *Julius Caesar* made you blush bright red,
and your spelling defeated us all.

In the music lesson you listened diligently for the beat
but never ever got it, though I can see you now
through the rehearsal room porthole window –

banging timpani, arms flailing wildly like someone drowning,
tip of your tongue curled round your upper lip,
eyes shut tight, banging and banging,

till someone complained, the way they always did complain
about you. Only your running blew them away,
your trainers' white soles flashing through the woods,
luminous then gone. *Where's he off to?* they'd mutter,

half-certain you were up to no good, then begrudging you
a little praise, then amazed at the speed of you

as you ran away, leaving the whole school behind you,
ran through tramlines of white paint on grass,
ran through summer – made air stand still,
ran into the sun (we put our hands across our eyes to watch you).

You took us with you to as far as we could go.
We saw you break the thin, white tape, still not believing.

Windswept

– their two heads turning, the wind licking up his hair,
blowing a curl straight across her forehead, startled
jubilance in both their eyes. His bank clerk shirt
a sudden white balloon, his tie with a life of its own
following the line of the river. Her fingers catching
playful at his fingers – casual, easy, just below the photo's
thin white edge. And behind them black and white England
glittering suddenly one springtime just after the war,
an elm tree shot with new leaves growing out of
their heads, curve of the valley, mirror flash of water.
Parked nearby, out of view, was surely that old blue Mayflower
waiting to trundle them towards the future:
both hands on the cake slice, *this is the picture
of the house we built*, twins in a pram with real spring
suspension, miles of sandcastles, nests of tables and
polished parquet floors, the endless ticking of a Sunday
lawnmower, *your mother and I think you ought to* . . .
But for now the young light catches them, the wind pulls
handfuls of clouds dizzily out of control.
She writes in her copperplate hand on the back
of the photo – *J & me, windswept.*

The Goodbye Letter

All day, writing to you, I watch the boys
trying to roller-skate down the street.
The ugly whirr of their wheels burns the asphalt,
they bump off the pavement, then the giddy build-up
of their speed, all flailing butterfly arms –
repeating, repeating the glory
of the almost. Their every success
so loudly signalled by claps, cheers,
fists balling the air, by their noisy determination
that this time they almost did it.
I can follow their progress with my eyes closed,
still wait every time for the successful silence
of wheels gliding smoothly down the street
and away . . . But their criss-crossing skids
make lines on my paper, their jeers
are in my head. They yell and yell
for hours, keep falling, lick their grazes
like mongrel dogs, scrap for praise; could be heroes
for so little. Then they unstrap their skates
and wobble unfamiliar on ordinary legs
into the dusk, toss a goodbye over their shoulder.
That last bit so strangely easy.

Henry Shukman

Train Robbers

We each put an ear to the rail Indian-style,
heard a hiss, an electric twang. A churn of engine
bounced off a hill – a tractor dawdling, a plane
crawling across the sky? The singing in the rails

began to seethe, ricochet from line to line: a hollow
knocking of mallets. Which way? Our pennies
and spoons lay taped to the ribbon where the iron
had worn to a shine. A horn stabbed a warning.

Which way? Drums clattered round our ears. There it was,
a thundering diesel, yellow face greased with mud,
its coaltrucks bulking round the bend of trees
like hurtling houses. Afterwards we searched the sleepers,

spotted a glint in the hardcore: a silver coin
thin as a leaf, all trace of its minting gone.
The spoons flattened into lollipops
you'd have cut your tongue on, hot to the touch.

The Cry

A cold night, but we've left the restaurant
because he wants to be walked – my son
buttoned against me in my jacket,
eyes screwed tight and leaking,
face crunched in a cry that won't stop,
that has me knee-deep in the pavement.
We pass a pub window lined with glasses,
someone's laughing inside. The cry
goes on. Outside the synagogue now,
all locked up, a motion-triggered light
flicks on. This isn't meant to be symbolic
but the moment doesn't escape me:
the two of us born outside the gates,
he wailing. His breath stutters, re-enters
the cry as if he knows: no prayerhouse,
no candles lighting the way, no wine
to sluice the passage of weeks.
But at last the milky lids come down.
He's come a long way, has a long way to go.

Adrian Slatcher

My Alien Problem

My alien problem first surfaced in between episodes of catatonia.
Because I have illness history, I realise how little I will be believed.
Were I a more trusty source, there would be plenty of interest.
My past record indicates a willingness to fabricate and make up things.
I have no need to do that, except I knowingly attention-seek.
In the past three years I have seen unicorns and been attacked by stigmata.
My vegetable tray resembles a tableau of saints.
Even my mother has stopped answering my calls.
Weird deaths happen to my immediate family.
The radio plays the tune that I am currently humming backwards.
Storms avoid our house for fear of being ignored.
Sometimes I can even sleep with the light on.
But, considering all this, think of your own life,
Is it that I am so strange?

Nostalgia

It was a difficult summer that year.
The artists had already left the building.
A plague of jellyfish covered the coastal towns.
All leave was cancelled for the sake of public order.
Here, as ever, the less that's said, the better
For a slow dog climbed the south road all day, then died.
Bad smells remained undetected in the suburbs
And a man was shot in the head whilst walking through the woods.
They say a rock shaped like an angel was seen to bleed.
I had become less enamoured of prescribed pastimes.
Got a reputation for hurting the weak, killing birds.
Last thing a mother needs at times like this.
The rationing had begun to take hold and it was hard
But for the best. Emergency procedures were set in place.
Soap and water remained the best of cures.
The word on the old woman was bad, but expected.
Each spring there would be less flowers than the one before.
We named each other for our least favourite animal.
Man that I was, I excelled at catastrophe.
The white witch fled town in fear for her life.
So goes it: bad things happen.
I first saw love arc over the opal bannister
And took to my bed with an acute bout of nostalgia.
But no wonder: who knew then how much we had lost?

Catherine Smith

Charades

Strangle Bully Delicious, you whisper in my ear.
Pretend it's a film. Go on. I throttle my own throat,
kick out. I mime guzzling ice-cream, dripping

with desire. You're making me grotesque, a freak
with bulging neck, gobstopper eyes,
lashing the audience while licking my lips;

they call out *Gladiator, The Nutty Professor,*
Frankenstein, Nine and a Half Weeks.
You cackle as my movements grow more frantic.

No-one guesses. *Tell us.* You hug me tight,
and our guilty secret hums like radiation
between us. Strangle. Bully. Delicious.

Postulant
For P.B.

The morning of her vows to Christ
Sister Patricia cracks a fertilized egg.
The chick's eyes are sealed tight,
head huge on its wizened body,
bright blood filming the yolk.

Later, scissors, then a razor
are wielded over her scalp,
leaving it coarse as a man's chin.
Her nape prickles in a draught.
Palms pressed, she kneels

and raises her eyes to the crucifix.
Today she'll be His bride,
shaved clean, a vessel for His will,
leached of desire. Metal
floods her saliva; she imagines

the chick's eyelids split open,
wings itching free, heaving itself
from the smashed shell,
its naked skull
bearing the dent of her spoon.

Absence

January 1971, Fletcher's Wood.
My jam-jar wriggling with tadpoles,
snot crusting my lip. I called

and you weren't there;
only my own breathing,
a rush of swollen river,

the quiet throb of damp earth.
I thought of your face under water,
hot piss stinging my legs.

Losing you in those days was easy:
refusing to play the game in the shed,
with the bandages and pegs

and your mum's *Paris Nights* lipstick.
Some days I asked for my dolls back.
You moved out of sight, then in.

Thirty years on, a dream
soaks my nights. I wake, shouting.
Your name dries on my lips.

You, but not you; a husk of you
washed blank by three day's river.
An absence of identifying marks.

Julian Stannard

The Red Zone

I need to get back into the Red Zone
because I left something in the apartment
ten, twenty, thirty years ago.
And this little row of pants lining the alleyway,
handwashed, sparkling . . .
I need to climb these slate stairs.
Has anyone bothered with the locks?
And I thought the city so quiet
until helicopters drifted over my shoulder.
I need to get into that apartment
with its high ceilings, its whorey curtains,
the bat still flapping in the wardrobe,
a baby on the table.
Did someone leave a baby on the table?

Mortlake
(1982)

Sometimes I gave Yiannis the slip.
I'd nip out into the kitchen yard,
a hefty chop of jiving maggots,
smoke a Marlborough and relax.
I'd wipe the oil up and down my apron.
Then I'd take a large brown egg out of the fridge
watch it lazing in my hand
and launch it sky-high above the wall,
the busy road, the station, Mortlake . . .

Peace

Our lives passed by in a state of desire.
Narrative of rubble, sob-shake of stones.
We hopped off trams, arranged the rendezvous.
The Tommies were kind but aloof, and the Yankees!
We loved the French for their manners.
One night we tampered with the wires for light.
There was no poverty under bedclothes.
The city was our children's kindergarten.
They grew up in six days with quick eyes.
One night we spilt champagne over a dress.
The city tottered, the elderly tottered.
Speeches of the Führer were sold under arches.
Ghosts were blown in with the dust.
Dust was blown in with the ghosts.

Ross Sutherland

Dear Grandma and Granddad

I am behind you in the corridor, pretending that I know you,
                                              calling you so and so.
You need to go and get the nurse to show the way back
                                              to your room
because I have moved it
I've swapped it, replaced it, half-unscrewed it. I have meddled
with all the locks and buried the keys beneath crazy paving.

You say: 'Lord, take me now. I am ready for saving.'
I am down in your patio
treading on your orchids, covering my fingers in dry soil.
I am lying to your neighbours, pissing on the linoleum
leaving on the television when you go to bed.

We are both armchair buddhists, and you cannot escape me
though you fight me with hairspray and knitting needles,
embroidered cushions, scented lavender,
calendars of puppies, wide-eyed and lovesick.

But I will return, like a man-shaped brick
thrown through your window in the middle of the night –
to burn your tinder bungalow down
will only take one light.

Rutger Hauer

my dad
hijacks a nuclear weapon
and threatens to launch it at washington
if his demands aren't met

he salutes a television wall
and consults the rest of
the terrorists
who whoop like monkeys
at his command

at the end of the film
when his army is defeated
he stands alone on his secret island
and stares into broken radar screens
sparks raining off his uniform

I pause the video

less than a second before
rutger hauer rolls out of the darkness
and puts his hands
around my father's throat

and edge the film on
frame by frame
until the director goes in for an extreme close-up
and my dad's eyes defocus
and his lips bleed food dye

and then I get down
on my hands and knees
press my face against the television set
and tell him that sometimes
it's okay to lose

Shelli Tape

Roses and Ashes

You sat behind a
bunch of roses with fingers
rested on the thorns,

that dried out old pipe
between your teeth. You couldn't
see me for petals

but instead watched
clear condensation run down
the window, hearing

drops fall and fizz like
lethal acid on the hot
radiator. You

left me wiping off
the white mist. The dumped roses
strewn on the bedside

table, their small heads
pressed against the boiling pipes,
shrivelling to chapped lips.

Fossil

Do you remember, Dad,
how perfect she looked
on that beach, barely clad
in knickers, her skin cooking

like blushed pink paper
under a glassy sun,
and how I studied her
silver bones in wonder

whilst the birds thought
she was a fossil and pecked
at her feet and head,

until you softly caught
hold of her wrist and regrettably
whispered she was dead.

Free from Porridge

I watched them, leaving
me to loll over the porridge,
to endure the trial alone.

My spoon ticked
around the bowl like a sun dial

cut to shreds by a Venetian blind.

I had an empty vanity case,
but I lined it with clotted milk.
They hung a plastic apron

around my neck
so I didn't waste a thing;

took away my sheet

because I wasn't dead,
so I couldn't hide an oat.
Instead I coughed porridge

up over my knees and feet,
until the spoon struck twelve.

I watched nurses float

over disinfectant floors,
lift me by the hair,
stop me choking.

I felt their palms pinch
inside my arm pits,

carry me, crucify me

along the sick corridor,
throw fingers down my throat.
I dropped the spoon.

Now time has stopped.
My skin bubbles over a needle

like grains of porridge.

Frances Thompson

Sewing at the Window

These trousers have hung in the wardrobe
for over half a year. Too long. Today
it's out with the scissors and the old biscuit tin
with needles and pins and tangled-up stuff in.

On the radio, *The Story of the Rose*.
It's a drop of Allah's sweat, sweetening
the faithful for worship. Idea of perfection.
Dead, Its breath lingers.

I cut and pin the legs, try the new length
twice, three times, before I'm satisfied.
Slow afternoon light and solitude
make perfection desirable, possible even.

Christian monks loved the rose, first of all
for the learning of its ways, next for its lending
new life to Mary of 'heile Bedlehem', and then
for the sublime geometry of rose windows.

The light is best by the window, obviously.
(In any other age, it wouldn't need to be said.)
Even so, threading the wretched needle
takes ages, a perfect exercise in patience.

Prayer-beads were counted in petals, hence the rosary.
The Church was shaken by *The Romance of the Rose*.
Where might the meaning of the heresy lead –
the scandal of Rose seduced, possessed?

Prick up just enough cloth to hold, not enough
to show, a firm wedge of the folded hem,
the right spacing and tension. Look, Miss Blackstock,
look at how neat I've been.

Roses are for war and peace and politics.
In York Minster, the red and the white intertwine,
in Scotland, roses and thistles. 'Make up,'
the rose is made to whisper, 'Vote New Labour.'

My sewing-machine has many functions –
a special arm with herringbone stitch for hems,
and a bright light. It remains
locked in its cupboard. For I am bound

by these threads into an ageless afternoon
with Lucy Snow and her tiny dots of blood;
with Great-Aunt Sarah, crippled, at her window,
crafting perfect leaves, fleurs-de-lys, roses.

Hymn

Glorious things of thee are spoken –
four sharps and a few hundred voices.
We rap it out like Cliff
off on his Summer Holiday,

Zion, City of our God –
the tune parts company with itself
smokey brick of Shankill from
Malone's cool hedges,

He whose word cannot be broken
unlike paving stones –
up a long ladder oh Zion City
and down a short rope,

Formed thee for his own abode –
so God save King Billy,
to hell with the Pope,
or vice versa, depending,

On the rock of ages founded –
hopscotch on the cracks,
and the Catholic kids dancing,
skittering off sideways,

What can break thy sure repose?
ask the canny tenors, as if they didn't know,
and the bank-boss basses, all security, they know all right,
and the lilting, tilting sopranos and altos in hair-do's,
lips twitching into half-smiles through their 'O's, all of them
sustaining what they know by mutual agreement
like a good moment in sex –

With salvation's walls surrounded –
shrill and sure, let go, make a joyful noise because
we're on the homeward run now and
Jesus bids us shine so he does
out of these very walls with a pure clear light,

Thou shalt smile at all thy foes.
That's that then.
AAAAAAA- (bring in the dominant and . . .)
men. Resolution. Rustle. Sit. Sermon.

Severance

The man who is splitting stones
says that the rock,
in the moment before it breaks,
speaks –
gives a leathery *Yes*
along its agreed lines
of surrender.

I thought of how,
when you slice a carrot
lengthways,
it springs apart from itself
as if it has been waiting
all of its life
for this relief.

Sometimes, says the man,
you get smooth stone,
that does not so much crack
as slide apart
in great curved slabs.
I saw cooked codflesh,
gleaming.

He feels
he is granting a favour
to the damp virgin rock-face,
that has not yet
been frosted with dew,
or salted, or crusted
with lichen.

She

Like some forgotten foundling ghost
the white-bodied woman stoops and creeps
stirring my settled waters.

I am stalked in the dark by stories –
not of flawed Achillean heroes, or unicorns,
or people of dreams –

she is of herself, trailing ash and verdigris,
moving in poppy, heliotrope, verbena,
and wind-blown marigold.

She will not rest.
I will not invite her to rest,
to stir tea in a cup.

She knows the Codling moth and the Comma
and the milkweed, and the small dimpling hand
that my mother knows.

I turn from her – we have no common talk.
When I look, she has slipped
back to the water.

Emily Wills

Appraisal

It's what you'd like to do
when you get round to it
in an ideal world, after the news
when you've fed the cat, changed
brown walls to white, tidied the desk,
wiped out the third world debt.

It's expected of you; always has been
slouched in the back row of your mind
these grass-is-greener days. Dreams
you used to darn are bagged,
car-booted: you're changing walls
for walls, wiping out the news.

It's what you promised yourself,
one day, next year, soon. It lies in wait
in black and white with teeth
and a speech bubble you can't quite see.
It's what you ought to want
to do, and now
it's written down.

Holes

*Some things, once you've got them
are difficult to get rid of.*
– Fleur Adcock

Holes in the ground, for instance. This one
has swallowed carpets, mattresses,
and rocks, fist-sized, thrown
because a mineshaft, like the sea
demands stones, thrown or skimmed
timed to measure thirty metres falling.

She, too, demanded stones
and parts of him, cast off. He loved
her hidden streams, the way
she swallowed his stories whole,
her sense of direction in the dark.

He filled her in. For a while
she was hole in the heart,
history, survivor. One night,
a tremor, low on the Richter scale
opens her exact, unmarked boundary,
ready for every fistful he chooses
to hurl, timing slowed seconds
stone's throw, gravity, bruise.

Mackerel Fields

In summer it's blue-tide
pink-thrifty, posing
for snapshot daytrippers
who dawdle the one up
one down terraced street
now window-boxed,
sea-viewed, with sheets
provided.

Marram grass erodes
to a car park, fun fair;
fishermen have left their nets,
their spring green fields,
and every high tide long
bright mackerel boats
shoal to the island and back
so the fishermen harvest
a sparse glittering of coins.

It's a grey place
in winter; head-scarved,
bent to salt wind. Bright paint
peeling, pinkwhite reverts
to granite, damp inside.
Boats dare further out now
scraping the barrel of the sea's hoard
though it cheapens, will not sell,
so the fishermen's fields
scale mackerel blue and silver
rotting, stinking on the wind.

Anna Woodford

Vena Amoris

Three little pearls
hang from each lobe,
they look like the real thing.

Pinned to your blouse
is a brooch
from another of his trips,

its gilt edge frames a lady's cameo,
her sideways glance
weighs heavy at your breast.

Your wrist is caught up
in a grand gesture of beads,
they hold their value –

despite the arrangement they're part of –
they touch you,
like all of his gifts,

the high price of each absence
brought home to you.
His excuses are made

in instalments of jewellery,
its silver-tongued prevarication,
its slight variation on a theme.

Set in this present tense,
your wedding band
is a design on forever.

It widens to a more generous understanding
than the one you first entered,
it hardens to understood.

Running underneath it
is the vena amoris,
the love vein

beneath the ring finger,
with no rational explanation,
a direct line to your heart.

Darling

I was nobody's darling,
everybody's pet,
except when Gran came up,
I was her duck.
Darling was for girls who weren't
that special, they were the non-speaking angels
in the nativity, their sandwiches cut into right angles,
their mothers ranging from affection to affectation
when they called them home
across the playground: 'Darling!'

Your mouth sums me up,
moving silently over my stomach,
singling out a thigh
but when you call me darling,
it's my mother's tongue in my head
that hushes you. I know it's only a word,
I knew, as a backseat driver, at seven,
my eyes screwing streetlights into stars,
that when we passed the sign for Darlington,
it wouldn't live up to its promise.

The Coliseum

The original floor of the Coliseum
has disappeared into myth,
it leaves a hole that time can't heal,
that new generations can't fill,
except with temporary solutions,
like the plank's loose footing
or the bridge's sidling tongue.
This is the space death leaves,
its enormity no less for one
than for all the gladiators that ran into this Arena,
the animals that were winched into it.
This is the thin air all endings are airbrushed into.
It is the bottom falling daily out the world.

Morgan Yasbincek

golden hands

she lives across the road from the
corn field, her house loosely penned
by animal runs and rooms her husband
has built on over years of weekends

he cuts down homemade salami from
the roof of one of these rooms
when his daughter visits
a froth of blue mould curves along its seam

when he's not home she sometimes
takes off her scarf and dances with
the turkeys, lifting feet in 'levi' mules, shaking
down a rain of grain and lettuce ends

she says these are her golden hands
the nails have blackened cracks down their length
she warms them in turkey blood, dishwater, spinach soup

she sits with her feet up on the bench and chews
the dry, dark orange corn, her golden teeth

horses and dragons

she won't let you drag her through
life like a limp, black-stockinged sheep

she can handle big animals, she says she
used to break them in

her body is no tetchy bird that hops out a neurosis
of chasing away, chasing away, chatty with fear
her soft heart hangs quietly, like the cheeks
of an old nana

she won't be siphoned, or find herself in some
scene involving other people's houses, beds or
telephones

you're no horse whisperer

look at you

london, with your
shaved boys, your candy buses, your black
corpuscles

your sleepless drag their blankets
lift them high off the wet pavement,
their clean dogs keep a solemn pace behind

in a west end alley restaurant the maître d'
greets all like a temple guardian, his palms
joined

a cluster of men in black and white tiger print
suits hatch from a black rolls royce

look at you, london, your body alive
with seduced australians, gardens and streetlight and
beautiful secret people in coats

underground, blue veins, red arteries of cable
frantically unravel alongside the speeding tube,
lives undone

look at you, you tight up price, you
scaly fin, you broke, hemmed up lush, all
malachite and cheap glitter

even the pigeons hurry to ground, race on foot, join
the rush into your bonfire

even they will make airborne confetti of themselves
just so they can be lit by you

my sister's cat

had purple marble for an eye and ate alone in a laundry which
always
held an odor of drying tinned fish, spice disinfectant and
washing powder
a sad place, a lonely place for a cat

he would squat over the bowl, crouch by the back door to eat
sometimes people would walk through and he'd withdraw a little
from the bowl
his tail would uncurl and he'd watch their calves as they
slammed the screen door
then he'd resettle into the hug of his curled tail, tap his nose on
the rim of his bowl

in other rooms we could hear his bowl shifting
in increments as he ate, ceramic scraping tiles
when it was taken for washing, he'd sniff the air above where
it would have been and walk away, expressionless

extinguish

when the tiger escapes from the zoo
they decide to keep it quiet

it has happened before, the animal
returned of its own accord
before anyone noticed –
all those bars, stripes, confuse the issue

with her arthritic hip and bad teeth she
can only ever be lost –
there are no campfires to pick out her
coat, no flames here to blend with

she isn't staring anyone down
like a dog let out after the ranger's
gone home

it's a cunning performance
– she calls herself princess taj mahal

Notes on Contributors

Liz Almond was born in Newcastle-upon-Tyne and now lives in Hebden Bridge. She teaches creative writing at Manchester Metropolitan University's Alsager Faculty. Her work has been published in magazines including *Ambit*, *Boomerang*, *Cyphers* and *Writing Women*. A first collection, *The Shut Drawer*, was published by Arc Publications in June 2002. The poem 'Game' won a prize in the Peterloo Poetry Competition 2002.

Steve Barker was an advertising copywriter for a dozen years and now runs a model agency. Before that, he read English at the University of Wales. He is currently working towards a first collection.

Alex Barr won third prize in the National Poetry Competition 2000. His poems have appeared in leading magazines in the UK, and also in Canada, Ireland, and the USA. His first collection, *Letting In The Carnival*, is published by Peterloo.

Paul Batchelor is a writer.

Anne Berkeley lives near Cambridge. She is a member of the poetry ensemble J6. She won the Blackwells/*Times Literary Supplement* prize in 2000. Poems have appeared in several magazines including boomeranguk.com, *The Interpreter's House*, *The North*, *Obsessed with Pipework*, *Orbis*, *The Rialto*, *Smiths Knoll*, *Staple* and *Tabla*. Her pamphlet *The buoyancy aid and other poems* was published by Flarestack in 1997.

Roy Blackman co-edits the poetry magazine *Smiths Knoll*, is an OCA writing-tutor and Secretary to the Aldeburgh Poetry Trust. A Hawthornden Fellow in 1993, his collection *As Lords Expected* (not about cricket), was published by Rockingham in 1996. A second collection and a pamphlet have followed and he will appear in the *Oxford Poets Anthology 2002*.

Lawrence Bradby was born in Glasgow, raised in Kent and started his working life in Cromer. He now lives in Norwich and teaches an Open Univeristy course on geology. He rarely travels without a map.

Peter Carpenter is a Visiting Arts Council Poetry Fellow at the University of Warwick; he is also the co-director of Worple Press, and Literary Editor to the Estate of William Hayward. *The Black-Out Book* (Arc, 2002) is his latest pamphlet, following the chapbook *No Age* (Shoestring, 2001). He is also the co-author of *At The End Of The Day*, a 'dictionary of received footballing wisdom.' He lives and works in Kent.

Emily Dening was born in London and lives in Cambridge. She has had a series of humdrum jobs allowing her time to develop creative energies. She's a member of the First Tuesday poetry group, and has had poems published in *Smiths Knoll* and *The Rialto*. She was also a runner-up in the Peterloo Open Poetry Competition 2001.

Josephine Dickinson was born in 1957, profoundly deaf from the age of six. She read Greats at Oxford, taught music for the next several years and became a composer. She then organized arts access projects in London before decamping to the high Pennines where she now lives with her ninety year old husband and assorted animals. Her first poetry collection, *Scarberry Hill*, was recently published by *The Rialto*.

Frank Dullaghan was born in Ireland and has been widely published in the UK and Ireland: *HU*, *London Magazine*, *New*

Welsh Review, *The North*, *Nimrod* (University of Tulsa, USA), *Poetry Ireland Review*, *The Rialto*, *The Shop* and *Thumbscrew* amongst many others. He has an MA with Distinction in Creative Writing from Glamorgan University, and is an ex-Editor of *Seam*. He is one of the organizers of the Essex Poetry Festival.

Margaret Easton grew up in Warwickshire. She graduated in English from the University of East Anglia. She lives in Suffolk and works as an analytic psychotherapist. Her poems have appeared in *Writing Women*, *Oxford Magazine* and *Smiths Knoll*.

Jo Ezekiel was born in Essex in 1969. For several years, she worked as a primary school teacher in East and South London. Her poems have been published or are forthcoming in a variety of magazines, including *Other Poetry* and *Poetry Nottingham*. She currently works as a bookseller and lives in South London.

Stuart Flynn was born in Australia in 1966 but has lived in London for a number of years. Once a City lawyer by profession, he now writes full-time. His poetry has been widely published in UK magazines and his first pamphlet, *Seneca the Spin Doctor*, was published in 2001 by Acumen Publications. His translations of poetry from Latin, Ancient Greek, Italian and German have appeared in many magazines and a book of poems translated from Latin is due in 2002.

T. K. Fountain was born in rural Georgia, USA, in 1972 and received an MA in English from The University of Memphis, Tennessee, in 1998. For four years he lived and taught in Ankara, Turkey. In 2001, a small selection of his poetry was published in the collection *Framing Reference* (Near East Books, 2001). Currently he lives in New York City and is the Book Reviews Editor of *Near East Review: A Journal of International Poetry and Literature*.

Ivy Garlitz was born in Florida and lived in Poland and Germany before settling in Britain. She gained her Ph.D. in

Creative and Critical Writing at the University of East Anglia where she now teaches literature and creative writing. A featured poet in *Thumbscrew*, her poems have appeared in *Poetry Review*, *The Rialto*, and other magazines. She was shortlisted for the 2000 Geoffrey Dearmer Prize. Her first pamphlet, *A Better Life*, is published by the Bay Press.

Anna Garry is from Ireland. She is a graduate of the MA in Creative Writing at UEA and has been published in *Critical Quarterly*, *Reactions 1* and *Birdsuit*. She lives in Norwich.

Margaret Gillio was born in Colorado and raised in rural Nevada. She taught contemporary fiction, poetry, and composition in Ankara, Turkey for three years and has recently returned to St. Paul, MN. She is currently working in a home for at-risk teenagers, as well as teaching online English courses for the University of Phoenix. Her work has been published in various North American literary magazines. In 2001 a collection of her poems was published in an anthology, *Framing Reference* (Near East Books, 2001).

Chrissie Gittins has published widely in magazines, newspapers, anthologies, and in two pamphlet collections. Her poems have also been broadcast on BBC Radio 4 and the BBC World Service. She has recently received awards from the Society of Authors and the Royal Literary Fund and in 2001 was awarded a Hawthornden fellowship. Her poetry for children appears in Macmillan, Pearson Education and Hodder Wayland anthologies. Her radio play *Starved for Love* will be broadcast by BBC Radio 4 on 25 October 2002. She is currently Poet-in-residence with 'gifted and talented' pupils in Southwark.

John Hatfield lives in York. He studied painting as a student and spends his time drawing, painting, and writing. John wrote and illustrated the series of *Quintilian* books for children, published by Jonathan Cape (now out of print). His poetry has been published in *Yorick*, *Poetry Review*, *Expression Poetry*

Quarterly. A group of poems, *Almanack*, was set to music by the distinguished composer David Blake. John studies languages, classical mythology, and has an absorbing interest in the work of John Ruskin.

Yannick Hill is about to graduate and will be staying in Norwich to do an MA in creative writing in September. His sister is amazing.

Patrick Hobbs was born in South America of English and Danish parents, but grew up in England. After a degree in History at Bristol University he worked with social services in London and Liverpool and spent some months making bread in a monastery before becoming a furniture-maker. Forced to abandon this because of illness, he has since set up and run an art gallery. His first collection of poems, *Paper Hands*, was published by Dancing Blue Press in April 2001. He now lives in Kent.

Andrea Holland did a Master of Fine Arts in Creative Writing in the U.S. and now teaches at UEA and at the Norwich School of Art & Design, where she edits the literary anthology, *Birdsuit*. She has poems in *New Writing 10*, *Reactions* volumes 1 and 2, *The Rialto*, *The Greensboro Review*, *Other Poetry*, *Ibid* and other U.S. journals.

Naomi Jaffa was born in 1961, grew up in London and North Yorkshire, and read English at Oxford. She lives with her partner on the Norfolk/Suffolk border and has worked for the Aldeburgh Poetry Trust for nearly ten years. Since 1999 she has been Director of the annual Aldeburgh Poetry Festival. Her poems have been published in *The North*, *The Rialto* and *Smiths Knoll*.

Christopher James holds an MA in Creative Writing from the University of East Anglia. He is widely published in magazines and anthologies and in June 2002 was a recipient of an Eric Gregory Award from the Society of Authors.

Brian Johnstone is a poet, photographer and creative writing tutor. He has been published in Scotland, England, Wales, Greece and Poland. His first collection is *The Lizard Silence* (Scottish Cultural Press, 1996), his most recent, *Robinson: A Journey* (Akros, 2000). He was awarded a Scottish Arts Council Writer's Bursary in 1998. He has won both the Mallard and Trewithen Poetry Competitions and in 2000 was 'Highly Commended' in the National Poetry Competition. He is currently Administrative Director of StAnza: Scotland's Poetry Festival and is employed as a creative writing tutor by St Andrews University Centre for Continuing Education.

Chris Kinsey lives in Powys. She received an Arts Council of Wales writer's award in 2000/1 and has been published in a variety of magazines, anthologies and on BBC Radio 4. She writes freelance, regularly runs sessions on 'writing & recovery' with people affected by mental illness and sometimes works in schools and with adults with learning difficulties.

Joel Lane lives in Birmingham. He is the author of a collection of short stories, *The Earth Wire* (Egerton Press, 1994); a collection of poems, *The Edge of the Screen* (Arc, 1999); and a novel, *From Blue To Black* (Serpent's Tail, 2000). He and Steve Bishop have edited an anthology of urban crime and suspense stories, *Birmingham Noir*, due from Tindal Street Press October 2002. His second novel, *The Blue Mask*, is due from Serpent's Tail in January 2003.

Brenda Lealman grew up in West Yorkshire and after many years further south now lives on the North Yorkshire Moors. Much of her poetic inspiration comes from northern landscapes and language; for instance *Nought at the Pole* (Flarestack, 1997) is a short sequence of poems based on her time living with the Inuit peoples of Baffin Island. She was a prizewinner in the Bridport Competition 1998; a runner-up in the *Staple* Open Competition 1998; and a winner in The Poetry Business Competition 1999. She had a collection, *Time You Left*, published by Smith/Doorstop in 1999.

V. G. Lee has been writing poetry for several years and in that time has had poems published in anthologies and magazines including *PLN* and *Poetry Review*. In 1999 Lee was shortlisted for *Poetry Review*'s 'Dearmer Prize'. She has published one novel, *The Comedienne* (Millivres Books, 2001).

Christine McNeill was born in Vienna, and has had one collection published, *Kissing the Night* (Bloodaxe, 1993). Her work has appeared widely in Britain, Ireland, and Australia. Next year Dedalus Press will be publishing her translation of Rilke's poem-cycle on *The Life of the Virgin Mary*. Another full-length translation of Rilke's *The Book of Hours* (with a Jungian interpretation) is currently looking for a publisher.

George Messo was born in 1969. His books include *From The Pine Observatory* (Halfacrown Books, 2000), *Framing Reference* (Near East Books, 2001) and *The Complete Poems of Jean Genet* (translated with Jeremy Reed, Intimacy Books, 2001). He was a translator-in-residence at the British Centre of Literary Translation in January 1994 and will be Hawthornden Fellow in Poetry for June/July 2002. He is the editor of the international journal *Near East Review* and teaches in the Faculty of Humanities & Letters at Bilkent University, Ankara, Turkey.

Jenny Morris was born in North Yorkshire. She paints and writes poems and fiction in Norwich. Her writing has been widely published in magazines and anthologies (including *Reactions* volumes 1 and 2).

Stephanie Norgate's radio plays *The Greatest Gift* and *Clive* have been broadcast on BBC Radio 4. Her stage plays have been performed on the London Fringe. Her poetry has been published in magazines and anthologies such as *The North* and the *Poems of the Decade Forward Anthology*. *Fireclay* (1999) was a winner in the Poetry Business Book and Pamphlet Competition, and more poems appeared in *Oxford Poets 2000* (Carcanet). Stephanie runs the MA in Creative Writing at University College, Chichester. She received a writer's award from South East Arts in 2000.

Matt Nunn is many things, amongst them a creative writing fellow at Warwick university and the poet-in-residence of Birmingham City Football Club. His first collection, *Apocalyptic Bubblegum*, is due any season now.

Rennie Parker was born in Leeds, and currently lives in Stamford, Lincolnshire. Her first collection, *Secret Villages* (Flambard, 2001), was included in the Forward Poetry Awards 2002. She has a Ph.D. on the poet/composer Ivor Gurney, and also writes criticism.

Dean Parkin was born in Suffolk and currently works for two poetry magazines, *The Rialto* and *Smiths Knoll*, and for the Aldeburgh Poetry Trust. His poems have appeared in many magazines such as *Boomerang, Other Poetry, Prop, Reactions², Seam* and *Smoke*.

Kate Rhodes was born in London in 1964. She studied English at university and holds a Ph.D. on the work of the American dramatist Tennessee Williams. She has taught at British and American universities and now works for the Open University. Her poems have been published in a range of magazines including *Poetry Review, The North, Interpreter's House, Smiths Knoll* and *Poetry Monthly*. In 2001 she was short-listed for the *Poetry Review* New Poet of the Year award.

Jacqui Rowe lives in Birmingham with her husband, teenage daughter and a large Münsterländer puppy. She is currently Training and Development Officer at the University of the First Age in Birmingham, on secondment from her job as head of English in a boys' school. Her poems have appeared in *The Interpreter's House, Smiths Knoll, Mslexia, Poetry Review* and *The Seat and Suitcase Poems*, an anthology published by Flarestack.

Robert Seatter has twice been 'Commended' in the National Poetry Competition, won first prize in the London Poetry competition (2000), and was shortlisted for the Forward Poetry

Prize ('Best Individual Poem') in 2002. In addition, his work has collected prizes in Peterloo, Housman, *Tabla* and York poetry competitions, among others. He is featured in *Anvil New Poets 3* (2001), *Chalkface Muse* (White Adder Press, 1999), *Reactions²* (Pen&inc, 2001), and the *Poetry Society Education Pack for Schools* (2001). His poems have also appeared in: *Poetry Wales, Ambit, Poetry London, Envoi, Staple, Stand, Smiths Knoll, Tabla* and *Blade*; on the British Council and BBC World Service websites, and on the London buses! He lives in London where he works at the BBC.

Henry Shukman won the *Daily Telegraph* Arvon Poetry Prize and a *Times Literary Supplement* Poetry Prize in 2000, and has received awards from the Arts Council of England and Southern Arts. He has worked as a trombonist, a trawlerman and a travel writer, and his first collection, *In Doctor No's Garden*, is published by Cape in August 2002.

Adrian Slatcher was born in Walsall in 1967. He studied English at Lancaster and and has worked in York, London and Manchester where he now lives, and where he studied on the MA in Novel Writing. He has published short stories and poems, as well as collaborating on various music, film and internet projects.

Catherine Smith was awarded a bursary in 1998 from South East Arts to work on her poetry. She won third prize in the collection category of the New Writer Poetry Prizes two years running, and in 2002 was awarded second prize. Her poems have been published in *The New Writer, Equinox, Smiths Knoll, The Rialto, Mslexia, Staple, The North, The Independent* and *The Express* and various poetry anthologies. Her first poetry collection, *The New Bride* (Smith/Doorstop, 2001), was short-listed for the Forward Prize for Best First Collection.

Julian Stannard was born in 1962 and was educated at the universities of Exeter and Oxford. From 1987-93 he taught at the University of Genoa and returned there in 2002. He also lectures in English at Suffolk College, a college of UEA. His writing has appeared in many magazines and journals including *PN Review, Rialto, Reactions*[2]*, First Pressings* (Faber) and *The Guardian*. Last year Peterloo Poets brought out *Rina's War*, a first collection. He has written a study of Fleur Adcock and is now preparing a book on Basil Bunting.

Ross Sutherland was born in Edinburgh in 1979. He has been previously published in *writing on drugs* and *The Eggbox*, and has recently co-edited a collection of new writing, *Rock*. He co-runs a poetry club and hosts a late-night radio programme. He now lives in Liverpool, predominantly in the third person.

Shelli Tape is a post-graduate English Student researching the representations of the female body and the innovation of traditional poetic forms in contemporary women's poetry. Her first collection of poems is a thematic portrayal of an individual's regression into the eating disorder anorexia, in which anorexia functions as a metaphor for the way she aims to silence and starve the body of a poem and its subject matter through the use of 'strict' poetic rhyme schemes and syllabic control. She experiments with the breakdown of traditional poetic forms in order to reflect the deterioration of the body.

Frances Thompson has been published regularly in magazines in England and Ireland. She was a runner-up in the 2001 Bridport Prize. She twice won the regional section of the National Poetry Competition, and is now its judge. She is currently taking an MA in Creative Writing at Exeter University. Born and educated in Belfast, she now lives in Devon with her partner and cat.

Emily Wills is a full-time parent and part-time GP. She is also involved in a 'Writing for Health' project in a surgery in Gloucestershire. Her first collection, *Diverting the Sea*, was published in 2000 by *The Rialto*.

Anna Woodford is 28 and lives in Newcastle-upon-Tyne. She has published a pamphlet of poetry, *The Higgins' Honeymoon* (Driftwood

Publications), and has been widely published in magazines. She was awarded a Northern Promise Award from New Writing North in 2001 and a residency at Tyrone Guthrie in 2002.

Morgan Yasbincek is a Western Australian writer. Her first collection of poetry, *night reversing*, won the 1997 Anne Elder Poetry Award and the 1997 Mary Gilmore Poetry Award. Her first novel, *liv*, was published by Fremantle Arts Centre Press in June 2000. In 1998 she travelled to the United Kingdom where she completed a residency at UEA. She teaches creative writing at Murdoch University and is currently taking a break from researching her Ph.D. to care for her baby daughter and develop her second collection of poetry.

The Litmus Test: Call for Submissions
Reactions⁴ 2003

Is your poetry acid or alkaline? As long as it isn't neutral, I'd like to hear from you . . .

The fourth edition of *Reactions* will appear in 2003. *Reactions* is a forum for new poetry by new poets. Submissions are therefore invited from writers who have had a first collection or pamphlet published (but not a second), and from those who have not yet reached that stage.

If you are interested in submitting work, please send five poems with an SAE to Esther Morgan at the School of English and American Studies, University of East Anglia, Norwich NR4 7TJ.

The poems you send:
- can be on any subject, in any style and of any length.
- should be written in English, but can be in translation.
- should be typed, with your name and address appearing clearly on each.
- must be your own original work.
- must not already be accepted for publication by any magazine (although poems which are due to appear in a first collection or anthology will be considered).
- should be accompanied by a covering letter which lists the titles of your poems, plus a short biography (of no more than 70 words).
- need to reach me no later than 31 March 2003.
- must be good.

Volumes 1 and 2 of *Reactions* are available for purchase directly from Pen&inc at the special price of £5 plus £1 p&p. Please send a cheque made payable to the University of East Anglia, (remembering to indicate which volume/s you are ordering) to: Sara Wingate Gray, Pen&inc, English and American Studies, University of East Anglia, Norwich, NR4 7TJ.

www.penandinc.co.uk

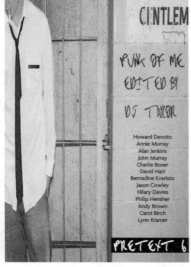

CINTLEM

PUNK OF ME
EDITED BY
DJ TAYLOR

Howard Devoto
Annie Murray
Alan Jenkins
John Murray
Charlie Boxer
David Hart
Bernadine Evaristo
Jason Cowley
Hilary Davies
Philip Hensher
Andy Brown
Carol Birch
Lynn Kramer

PRETEXT 6

Subscribe to UEA's new International Literary Magazine **Pretext** and get a back issue free. Published twice a year, **Pretext** aims to become one of the most exciting and innovative new literary magazines on the market.

Pretext 6 is published November 2002. It contains new fiction from Carol Birch, Bernadine Evaristo, Charlie Boxer and Annie Murray; new poetry from Alan Jenkins and Hilary Davies; an email exchange between DJ Taylor and Philip Hensher on experimentalism and the novel; an essay by John Murray on regional writing; Jason Cowley's exploration of his role as the literary editor for the *New Statesman* and lyrics by Howard Devoto of Buzzcocks' fame. **Pretext 6** also introduces fiction and poetry by emergent writers, Andy Brown, Lynn Kramer and David Hart.

Annual subscription costs only £14 including p&p, instead of the RRP of £7.99 per issue.
Send or email your name and address to:

**Emma Forsberg, Pretext Subscriptions,
English and American Studies,
University of East Anglia,
Norwich, NR4 7TJ
emma@penandinc.co.uk
www.penandinc.co.uk**

Pretext 6 is available in all good bookshops
from November 2002.